MICHA̶ ̶ ̶F̶O̶O̶T̶E̶

The BLOOMSBURY SET

HOMOSEXUAL RENAISSANCE

Cover photo: Paul Roche by Duncan Grant, circa 1945.

© 2017

"It was a thrilling moment, the coming together of a circle of glittering talents who would help to refashion England's literary and artistic culture for the next forty years, dragging it into the world of Modern."
Bloomsbury Set writer David Boyd Haycock

Heterosexual Paul Roche, the painting of whom is on the cover of this book, said in an interview about his relationship with the Bloomsbury homosexual painter Duncan Grant: "What can a homosexual do for a heterosexual? One thing he could do was save me the bother of finding a girl to make love to, the craze to find a woman would be put off for the time being. My need for sex was insatiable. He could suck or jerk me off and save me the sheer tedium of girl hunting, though the girl hunting resumed the moment he left."

"They were not a group, but a number of very different individuals, who shared certain attitudes to life, and happened to be friends or lovers. To say they were unconventional suggests deliberate flouting of rules; it was rather that they were quite uninterested in conventions, but passionately in ideas. Generally speaking they were left-wing, atheists, pacifists in the First World War, lovers of the arts and travel, avid readers, Francophiles. Apart from the various occupations such as writing, painting, economics, which they pursued with dedication, what they enjoyed most was talk--talk of every description, from the most abstract to the most hilariously ribald and profane."
Francis Marshall, present from the founding of the Bloomsbury Set.

"Whatever happens, I shall never be alone. I shall always have a boy, a railway fare, or a revolution."
Stephen Spender

"We repudiated general rules. We repudiated customary morals, conventions and traditional wisdom. We were, in the strict sense of the

term, immoralists."
Maynard Keynes and the Bloomsbury Set

"I immediately posed nude for Duncan who kissed each piece of clothing as I took it off, and each piece as I put it back on."
Paul Roche on Duncan Grant

"God, the immortality of the soul, redemption, the 'beyond' were concepts I had no time to pay attention to--not even as a child, perhaps because I wasn't childish enough. I was too curious, too questioning, too exuberant to put up with a concept as crude as the existence of a god. For me, God was an invitation *to not think*."
Nietzsche, important in freeing the minds of Bloomsbury members

My books include: *Cellini, Caravaggio, Cesare Borgia, Renaissance Murders, TROY, ARGO, Greek Homosexuality, Roman Homosexuality, Renaissance Homosexuality, Alcibiades the Schoolboy, RENT BOYS, Buckingham, Homoerotic Art (in full color), Sailors and Homosexuality, The Essence of Being Gay, John (Jack) Nicholson, THE SACRED BAND, Prussian Homosexuality, Gay Genius, SPARTA, Charles XII of Sweden, Mediterranean Homosexual Pleasure, CAPRI, Boarding School Homosexuality, American Homosexual Giants, HUSTLERS* and *Christ has his John, I have my George: The History of British Homosexuality*. I live in the South of France.

CONTENTS

Page 95

CHAPTER TEN
Duncan Grant
Page 109

SOURCES
Page 143

INDEX
Page 147

§§

CHAPTER ONE

AN OVERVIEW

To understand the Bloomsbury Set one must understand the French expression *panier de crabes*, a basket of crabs, crawling over and through each other, copulating, yes, but also biting, their claws fully deployed. It was a sect where the sexes intersected, said a member, promiscuous to a degree unknown to even the Renaissance Borgias. Vanessa Bell begged the immensely handsome artist Duncan Grant to provide the seed to produce a child, which he did while also sleeping with Vanessa's husband Clive, as well as writer David Garnett who, looking down at Duncan's baby in her crib, vowed he would marry her, thusly prolonging his nearness to her father Duncan, a vow he kept [she would later have other lovers who were also sleeping with her at the same time they were with her father Duncan and with her husband Garnett]. The members of the Bloomsbury Set were writers and poets, artists and philosophers, basically atheists and pacifists utterly convinced they were the intellectual center of the world. The intersection of their sexes went far beyond playing musical beds. Their love and devotion was so deep that women married the men who were sleeping with the men they really loved, in order, like Garnett with Duncan's child, to be in proximity to the men too homosexual to sleep with them. The women were also known to commit suicide when the man they loved died, as did Dora Carrington who shot herself following the death of Lytton Strachey, and even Virginia Woolf loaded a coat with stones and walked into a river [a suicide based on multiple causes].

David Garnett, a photograph taken by Duncan who used the photos later as inspiration for his paintings.

A perfect example of Bloomsbury sexuality, then, was Duncan Grant's relationship with Vanessa Bell, the wife of Clive Bell. Duncan, a painter and a homosexual who had had exclusively homosexual encounters in boarding schools and elsewhere since puberty, decided to live with Vanessa whose husband was off elsewhere with mistresses. Vanessa [the sister of Virginia Woolf] badly wanted a child from the supremely good-looking and talented Duncan, who agreed to move in with her for the time needed to get her pregnant, after which sexual relations immediately ceased. Their little girl, Angelica, was given Bell's name, Bell who pretended to be her father.

Duncan Grant, 1885-1978.

Duncan stayed on with Vanessa for 40 years, which in no way inhibited his taking numerous lovers until her death in 1961 lightened his conscience. Paul Roche, the love of the second half of Duncan's life, said in an interview that before Vanessa's death Duncan had said he ''was desperate to get free of [the affair] and I remember on one occasion he was talking to Macdonald and to me, in Bond Street; that was the day he decided that he wasn't expected anymore to feel guilty about not making love to Vanessa. He felt so free as a result.'' The 40 years Duncan and Vanessa spent together, as the reader will see in Duncan's chapter, were years of mutual travel, painting side by side, a deep friendship that went far beyond a mere marriage.

David Garnett was present at the birth of Duncan's daughter, as said, and wrote a letter to a friend in which he stated, ''I think of marrying it. When she is 20, I shall be 46--will it be scandalous?'' It was. Garnett was thusly fucking the father *and* the father's daughter [although *presumably* not at the same time], something she found out later in life. She had four daughters with Garnett, one of whom had a role in Harold Pinter's *The Go-Between* and drowned in the Thames at age 29, another who would marry the son of Ralph Partridge, Ralph having been one of Lytton Strachey's lovers, about whom we'll soon have much to say.

Duncan, Duncan's daughter Angelica, and her brother Quentin Bell.

Born Vanessa Stephen, 1879-1961, Vanessa entered a family that included her sister Virginia, two brothers, Thoby Stephen and Adrian Stephen, and two half-brothers, George and Gerald Duckworth [her mother née Julia Duckworth], stepbrothers who used both Vanessa and her sister Virginia sexually when they were children and teenagers, almost a natural introduction into what would be the Bloomsbury Set's mores. The children were educated at home in languages, mathematics and history, and later Vanessa took up painting at the Royal Academy. After her parents' deaths she sold the family home and moved to Bloomsbury where she started a salon of artists and writers, among them Duncan Grant and Lytton Strachey, Leonard Woolf, the future husband of her sister Virginia, and Roger Fry. In addition to Angelica--her child with Duncan Grant--she had two sons with Clive Bell: Julian killed at age 29 in the Spanish Civil War, and Quentin who became a writer. Clive Bell also had sexual relations with Duncan Grant and Roger Fry [all prep-school boys were broken in homosexually years before their first contact with a girl, and so even basically heterosexual boys continued male-male copulation, an enormous timesaver when one was horny and looking for fast, uncomplicated relief (2)].

Duncan would live and travel with Vanessa for forty years [horrible photo but true companionship].

As for the stepbrothers, George Duckworth became a powerful public servant and was knighted. He had three sons. Gerald became a publisher and despite having abused both of his stepsisters he helped Virginia publish her first two novels at Hogarth Press, before he founded his own company, still existent.

Julian Bell, 1908-1937, became a Cambridge educated poet, a member of the Apostles, a friend of the Cambridge-Four [the spies Maclean, Burgess, Blunt and Philby] and was even Blunt's lover, to the immense jealously of Burgess who was smitten by the boy [the Apostles and the Cambridge-Four are covered in the following chapter].

Julian Bell

A pacifist, Julian wrote *We Did Not Fight*, an anthology of the memoirs of conscientious objectors. Even so, he wanted to serve as a soldier on the Republican side of the Spanish Civil War but his mother and his aunt Virginia Woolf persuaded him to take part in the less dangerous role of an ambulance driver. It was in the midst of helping the wounded that he was killed by bomb shrapnel.

Quentin Bell, 1910-1996, wrote, among other books, the highly lauded life of his aunt in two volumes, *Virginia Woolf: A Biography*. He taught art history at the University of Durham and was professor of Fine Arts at the Universities of Leeds, Oxford and Sussex. He named his son after his brother Julian, and died at age 86.

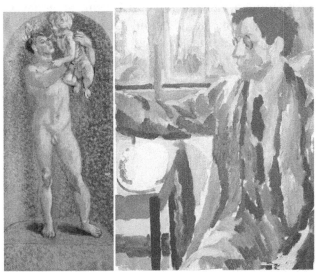

A joint painting of Duncan Grant by Grant and Vanessa, and Vanessa's painting of Duncan. Vanessa was considered an accomplish artist. She knew Duncan's lover Paul Roche and was said to have been both passionately jealous of Roche and passionately drawn to Roche's beauty, Roche who was at times her model [and most probably her occasional lover as he claimed he was heterosexual and because she had stopped sleeping with Duncan after her pregnancy].

Clive Bell, 1881-1964, was wealthy thanks to family coalmines. He was educated at Marlborough and Trinity College, Cambridge, where he studied history, good enough to win a scholarship to study in Paris where his interest in art led to his becoming an art critic. He was said to have been a snob, hedonist, womanizer, anti-Semite but not homophobe, fortune due to his love affairs with Grant, Fry and others. He became a pacifist, declaring that ''the worst tyranny is better than the best war,'' although he later forcefully backed Britain's war against Hitler.

David Garnett by Duncan.

Maynard Keynes said Duncan Grant had been the love of his life. From his youth Duncan had been one of Lytton Strachey's lovers, Strachey who was also his cousin. In addition, Duncan was the lover of Arthur Hobhouse. Hobhouse entered Eton at age 11, and then Balliol College, Oxford, seven years later. He had his own law practice, was on the board of a charity commission, worked as a law member for the council of the Governor-General of India, and was on the Judicial Committee of the Privy Council when he returned from India to London. He received a peerage as Baron Hobhouse, married and died without children, but during his youth *everyone* tried to bed him.

Duncan Grant with Keynes and a rare picture of Hobhouse, called Hobby, said to have been a beauty. At the time there were three irresistible lovers: Rupert Brooke, and a tie between Hobhouse and Duncan.

Duncan was accompanied during his later life by Paul Roche and Paul was at his side when he died.

Roche by Duncan Grant.

Duncan was born in 1885, just six months before the passing of the Criminal Law Act that criminalized male homosexual acts in England, regardless of consent, an act used to convict Oscar Wilde in 1895 (4). It was also dubbed the blackmailer's act because it was profitably used by hundreds of blackmailers afterwards. The fear of discovery was such that even later writers on Greek love, such as A.L. Rowse and Kenneth Dover, emphasized that they were happily married [which, conceivably, could have been true, despite evident homosexual leanings].

Paul Roche by Duncan.

Duncan went to prep schools in Rugby and London before entering the Westminster School of Art at age 17.

Paul Roche and perhaps an example of boarding-school fun, by Duncan Grant.

Leigh Farnell, one of Duncan's very first boarding-school friends, with whom he remained close all his life.

Duncan was unanimously described as charming and those who cared for him at the end of his life found him "impishly benign", despite active sex with boys who could have been his grandsons, and this throughout his entire eighties. He admired the philosopher G. E. Moore and told the boys who gave access to his old hands that he owed all of his moral philosophy to

Moore, ''which possibly does not amount to much'', said he [which was true, as Moore would never have approved of his promiscuity].

Duncan Grant by himself.

David Garnett, Grant's lover and Angelica's husband, was called Bunny since his childhood due to a rabbit cloak given to him then. When he married Angelica her parents were said to have been scandalized [although *which* parents, Vanessa and Bell or Vanessa and Grant, is not clear]. Garnett was an author, founded Nonesuch Press and ran a bookshop. From a first wife he had had two sons and with Angelica he had four daughters before they separated. He died in France in 1981 at age 89. Due to his central position in the Bloomsbury Set, he will have his own chapter later on.

Grant and David Garnett.

Paul Roche

Everything we learn about the Bloomsbury Set is astonishing and exceptional, and the friendship between Paul Roche and Duncan Grant amplifies the kinds of unique relationships that existed only in that grouping.

Paul and Duncan saw each other for the first time in 1946 while crossing Piccadilly Circus, apparently hazardous because when they made it to the sidewalk Paul said to Duncan, ''That was difficult'', to which Duncan answered, ''Indeed, it was,'' the first words in a companionship that lasted 32 years, until Duncan's death at age 93. Paul was handsome, in his mid-twenties, although ''I could be taken for 18'', while Duncan was 61 and, according to Paul, looked even older. Duncan invited Paul to his studio where they talked, where Paul agreed to pose for Duncan, where they made first love. Paul would become known for his love affairs with women, stating that the erogenous zones expertly caressed by Duncan stimulated him heterosexually so that afterwards he would go off in lusty pursuit of girls.

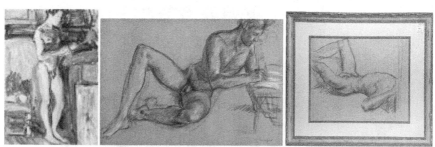

Three drawings of Paul Roche by Duncan Grant.

Paul claimed to have been heterosexual, the homosexuality of his young years in boarding schools having been situational, and his preference for wearing sailor suits could have been the fruit of his unfulfilled wish to join the navy, and not a come-hither to men who found him cute and sexually irresistible when so dressed, as Roche also found himself to be. It was certainly the reason why Duncan wrote his short *Patroclus and Narcissus*, Duncan taking himself for Patroclus who educated narcistic Paul, as stated by Roche: ''I was basically uneducated. I'd never been to the

14

ballet or the opera, or concerts or anything which is part of being a cultured person. So what Duncan did for me was to complete my education, and reading too. We went to a whole series of operas being done in London and ballet: the Ballets Russes played in London, and I was very, very struck by the Ballets Russes.''

Roche by Grant

Paul loved being the center of Duncan's attentions, Duncan's lust for his body exciting Paul enough for him to be able to respond sexually. When asked in an interview about their lovemaking, Roche's response was extraordinarily frank: ''So what can a homosexual do for a heterosexual? One thing he could do was save me the bother of finding a girl to make love to ... the craze to find a woman would be put off for the time being. That's what a heterosexual can be given by a homosexual. You see, I had no sexual feelings whatsoever towards Duncan. I know he was charming, good-looking and I loved him more than anyone on this earth but as for having any kind of direct sex with him, no. You see Duncan was such an honest person, and one of the last things he said to me, either before or after the big Paris exhibition of Cézanne--and he said it at least twenty or thirty or forty times in his lifetime--was 'I suppose you know that I love you?' And then another time, he said, 'As for anything sexual, forget about it, it wasn't really about sex at all, our relationship ... that's a side-track, nothing to do with what I felt for you and you came to feel for me.' He made that very clear.''

Paul by Duncan Grant

When they met in 1946 Roche had already been an ordained priest for three years, having been prepared for the priesthood in the Jesuit English College, part of the Pontifical Gregorian University of Rome, in 1943. He would continue on as a practicing curate through his affair with Duncan and with numerous women until he left the priesthood in the 1950s. He married twice, fathering two boys and two girls with his second wife, Clarissa Tanner, whom he married in 1954, and a son, Tobit, with a lover, Mary Blundell, a little earlier.

It was Duncan who suggested that Roche take up writing, and he began turning out books, all the while posing for Duncan, including his role as Christ:

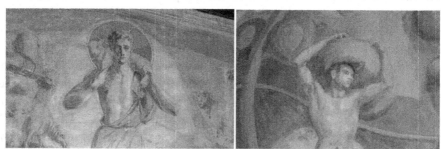

Paul as Christ in Grant's Russell Chantry, Lincoln Cathedral mural, where Paul shares space with another of Grant's models pictured here.

The modeling lasted for several decades, during which Paul would be stopped by the military police who would confiscate his sailor suits, but, said Roche in the interview, ''I always managed to find somewhere to buy another one'' [he was wearing it the day he met Duncan].

All Things Considered

PAUL
ROCHE

Paul produced several collections of poems, the most noted *All Things Considered* and *To Tell the Truth*, but he was especially known for his translations of Greek and Latin classics, Aeschylus, Sophocles, Aristophanes and Euripides. His Oedipus Rex was made into a 1968 film with Christopher Plummer and Orson Welles, the screenplay by Roche [with Duncan nearby drawing everyone who caught his eye]. Just as Duncan was given the title of the founder of the Bloomsbury Set, Roche was known as its poet. Roche had been born in India, his father an engineer who worked on the Great Indian Peninsular Railways, his mother dead when Roche was 9, of smallpox. From his youth he had been captivated by Catholic ritual, the reason he entered the orders, a calling that not only didn't survive Paul's lust for sex, but left him free to please Duncan. He gave up his religious calling after finding financial stability as a writer, translator and professor of English in several American colleges. He traveled extensively, often with Duncan.

Paul Roche will return, to bring closer to this book.

Paul by Duncan

The Set was against what Roger Fry [who had been the lover of Vanessa Bell, her husband Clive Bell and Duncan Grant] called Post-Impressionists, although Fry, an artist and art critic, defended them. Loved by many Bloomsbury members, male and female, he claimed he was basically heterosexual [his great love having been Vanessa Bell]. His list of Post-Impressionists included Cézanne, Gauguin, van Gogh and Seurat, to which he later added Rousseau and Toulouse-Lautrec. Many of the Set thought the Post-Impressionists were trivial in their art, reducing objects to basic shapes, while Seurat even painted tiny dots that some called Scientific-Impressionism. Van Gogh used lavish brush strokes to convey his feelings and states of mind, and Cézanne tried to bring purity in his art by reducing objects to basic shapes.

Roger Fry self-portrait and photographed by Duncan Grant.

Lytton Strachey, one of the founders of the Bloomsbury Set, seduced them all, even when he grew the beard he was so proud of, but that most others found ridiculous [and when the Bloomsbury Set didn't suffice for boys, he took control of the Apostles, adding vastly to his sexual wellbeing due to the boys who wanted entry, and those on the periphery who took part in Apostle debates and other activities].

One of 13 children, Lytton is the 3rd from the left.

Perhaps Roy Campbell, a poet and satirist, had Strachey in mind when he said that the Set was a group of "sexless folk whose sexes intersect". Some, happily, were far from being sexless. Duncan Grant was gorgeous, and when Strachey had intercourse with him he said that he felt joy because Grant was so moved and that what he loved "more than the consummation of my own poor pleasure ... was that for the first time I loved his soul," a need by the Set to introduce religion, philosophy and Plato somewhere in their sexual musical beds and bedrooms. As a lad Strachey justified sex by saying that "I may be sinning, but I am doing it in the company of Greece" in reference to Socrates and Greek texts on Hellenic love [homoerotic texts tutors were using to soften up their students for their private tutorials, and this in every prep school in England as well as Cambridge and Oxford (2).] Strachey goes on and on about the ideal love, the meeting of the minds, but Roger Senhouse, a student of Eton and Oxford University and owner of the publishing house that published Colette, Orwell and Günter Grass, said his relationship with Strachey had been sadomasochistic. In the same way, Plato went on about Platonic love, stating that "evil is the vulgar lover who loves the body rather than the soul," yet Plato and Socrates had nonetheless special permission to attend the athletic preparation of boys, where adults were banned by law, to enjoy the beauty of youthful dicks with their first pubic down and hairless asses (5).

Strachey, 1880-1932: He was proud of the reddish hue of his beard.

Strachey wrote a book *Ermyntrude and Esmeralda* in 1913, published in 1969, long after his death, in which two innocent girls titter about the "absurd little things that men have in statues between their legs." When the girls asked a priest what love is, he replies "the sanctification of something", unless the object is a member of the same sex. The book continues with a father who banishes his son for having sex with his tutor. But the son claims that he was only doing what the Athenians did and, anyway, his father "had done the same when he was a boy in school but had forgotten about it.''

Strachey's school was Trinity College, Cambridge, where he had sexual relations with Clive Bell who married Vanessa who would soon have sexual relations with Duncan Grant who had sexual relations with Strachey and David Garnett, Garnett who had sexual relations with Duncan Grant and, later, Grant's daughter Angelica, as reported [perhaps a smidgen too often]. Vanessa was no prude. She once told Maynard Keynes that he was so open, so human, that "One can talk of fucking and Sodomy and sucking and bushes and all without turning a hair."

Strachey was considered a joint founder--with Duncan Grant, Roger Fry, the Stephen brothers and Vanessa Bell--of the Bloomsbury Set. Bloomsbury was a location in central London encompassing Gordon and Fitzroy Squares. The aim of Bloomsbury was "to get a maximum of pleasure out of their personal relations. If this meant triangles or more complicated geographical figures, well then, one accepted that too." The Set existed in concert with the Apostles who met weekly over coffee and "whales" [sardines on toast] to discuss a topic later thrown open to discussion. Former members were angels, new members embryos. The bond between them all was lifelong. The spies Burgess, MacLean and Philby were Apostles.

Strachey's hallmark was biography, combining psychology with sympathy for the subject, irreverence and wit. He wrote *Queen Victoria, Eminent Victorians* and *Elizabeth and Essex,* a book that put the Virgin Queen in the company of a virile young man, all of which made him financially independent. When Strachey, a pacifist, was asked what he would do if a Hun tried to rape his sister, he answered: "I would insert my body between them." While others seduced girls by making them laugh, he did so through spellbinding eloquence [maintained his admirers].

In another of those strange Bloomsbury multi-faceted sexual relationships, Lytton Strachey lived with Dora Carrington who adored him and she married *his* lover Ralph Partridge, not for love, but to bring Strachey closer to her. Strachey was also "seeing" many other men, one of whom was Roger Senhouse whose sadomasochistic sex with Strachey included mock crucifixions [Senhouse is believed to have been Strachey's last lover]. Strachey paid for the marriage between Carrington and Partridge and, naturally, accompanied them on their honeymoon to Venice.

Later Carrington sent a moving letter to Strachey: "So now I shall never tell you I do care again. It goes after today somewhere deep down inside me, and I'll not resurrect it to hurt either you or Ralph. Never again. He knows I'm not in love with him. I cried last night to think of a savage cynical fate which had made it impossible for my love ever to be used by you. You never knew, or never will know the very big and devastating love

I had for you. I shall be with you in two weeks, how lovely that will be. And this summer we shall all be very happy together.'' Strachey wrote back, ''You *do* know very well that I love you as something more than a friend, you angelic creature, whose goodness to me has made me happy for years, and whose presence in my life has been and always will be, one of the most important things in my life.''

An example of Dora's work.

David Garnett described the relationship between Dora and Lytton: ''They became lovers, but physical love was made difficult and became impossible. The trouble on Lytton's side was his diffidence and feeling of inadequacy, and his being perpetually attracted by young men; and on Carrington's side her intense dislike of being a woman, which gave her a feeling of inferiority so that a normal and joyful relationship was next to impossible. When sexual love became difficult each of them tried to compensate for what the other could not give in a series of love affairs.'' Lytton had nonetheless deflowered Dora.

One of Carrington's compensatory affairs was with another of Partridge's lovers, Gerald Brenan. Brenan, 1894-1987, had been introduced into the Bloomsbury Set by Ralph Partridge's lover John Hope-Johnstone with whom, at age 18, Brenan planned to walk to China. At the end of 1,560 miles Brenan and John were forced to turn back due to lack of funds. Brenan took part in W.W. I. He met Carrington and Ralph in 1919 at age 25, later married, became a writer, and died at age 93 in a home attached to Hope-Johnstone's cottage, John who died at age 87.

Two photos of Brenan by his lover John Hope-Johnstone, but, alas, there is no photo of Hope-Johnstone in his youth.

Strachey bought the newly-weds a house and although Partridge was said to have genuinely loved Carrington, he left her for another woman and Carrington became pregnant by another man, Bernard ''Beakus'' Penrose, who asked her to leave Partridge [and, especially, Strachey]. She chose instead to abort.

John Strachey [Lytton's brother] and ''Beakus''.

Carrington's art received no critical attention, in part because she rarely had exhibitions and she didn't sign her work. Partially bisexual and physically androgynous, Virginia Woolf described her as eager to please, conciliatory, restless, inquisitive, impossible to dislike.

Around this time Aldous Huxley fell in love with her, ''Her short hair, clipped like a page's.... She had large blue china eyes ... of puzzled earnestness.''

Carrington, 1893-1932, and Lytton Strachey, seated, 1880-1932; Huxley and Senhouse. Roger Senhouse, 1899-1970, had had a sadomasochistic relationship with Lytton Strachey, had been Lytton's last lover and had been the lover of Michael Davies, who died in a suicide pact with Rupert Buxton. He was a publisher and translator, known for his translation and publication of Colette's *Cheri*, her *chef d'oeuvre*. He also published the works of George Orwell, *1984* and *Animal Farm.*

The woman Ralph Partridge finally left both Carrington and Strachey for was Frances Marshall, who took up with Ralph because she knew he was Strachey's lover, and as she loved Strachey she thought her proximity with Ralph would bring her closer to Strachey [a carbon copy of Carrington's reason for marrying Ralph].

Strachey and Partridge.

On his deathbed Strachey said, ''I always wanted to marry Carrington and I never did," words he hoped would consol her, although his biographer wrote that he had never planned any such thing. He did leave her £10,000 when he died at age 51 from stomach cancer, a fortune, but not enough to keep her from borrowing a revolver she used to commit suicide a month after Strachey's death. Strachey must have been a force of nature because he was a character in nearly all the books his friends wrote before and after his passing.

The intrigue doesn't end here: Painter Mark Gertler had also adored Carrington, to the point of obsession. Incapable of understanding why she preferred homosexuals to him, he bought a revolver and threatened to kill himself when she married Strachey's lover Ralph Partridge. [Dora did give herself to Gertler after making him wait in randy expectation for years, assuring him he was the first, although Strachey had had the honor a month earlier.] Gertler did finally commit suicide in 1939 at age 48, seven years after Carrington's death.

Mark Gertler, 1891-1939, said to have been a beauty.

In her diary Virginia Woolf wrote that she was glad to be alive and couldn't imagine why Carrington had killed herself. Ten years later, in 1941, Virginia did the same, by drowning.

Ralph Partridge was called the major by the Bloomsbury Set because of the way he perfectly filled out a uniform. Supremely masculine, some members were at first unsure as to how he would fit in with the group, but, sexually versatile, the answer was extremely well. Lytton Strachey was immediately smitten by him when Dora Carrington made the presentations. Ralph had been the rowing companion of Carrington's brother Noel at Christ Church, and had indeed reached the rank of major in the First World War. While Strachey found him supremely handsome, Carrington wrote Lytton this description, before he'd laid eyes on him: "Partridge shared all the best views of democracy and social reform. I hope I shall see him again--not very attractive to look at. Immensely big. But full of wit, and recklessness." Strachey wrote back asking her in what way he was "big". He soon found out for himself.

Strachey fell in love with Ralph and Ralph with Dora, but beyond sex the mutual friendships the Bloomsbury Setters formed lasted their entire lives, their promiscuous infidelities included. Strachey biographer Stanford Rozenbaum wrote, "A polygonal ménage that survived the various affairs of both without destroying the deep love that lasted the rest of their lives. Strachey's relation to Carrington was partly paternal; he gave her a literary education while she painted and managed the household. Ralph Partridge became indispensable to both Strachey, who had deeply loved him, and Carrington."

A member of the Bloomsbury Set who knew them all intimately, Francis Marshall wrote this observation in her *Memoirs*, which well summarized the Set: "They were not a group, but a number of very different individuals, who shared certain attitudes to life, and happened to be friends or lovers. To say they were unconventional suggests deliberate flouting of rules; it was rather that they were quite uninterested in conventions, but passionately in ideas. Generally speaking they were left-wing, atheists, pacifists in the First World War, lovers of the arts and travel, avid readers, Francophiles. Apart from the various occupations such as writing, painting, economics, which they pursued with dedication, what they enjoyed most was talk--talk of every description, from the most abstract to the most hilariously ribald and profane."

About Carrington's relationship with Ralph, Frances Marshall again says it best: "Her love for Lytton was the focus of her adult life, but she was by no means indifferent to the charms of young men, or of young women either for that matter; she was full of life and loved fun, but nothing must interfere with her all-important relation to Lytton. So, though she responded to Ralph's adoration, she at first did her best to divert him from his desire to marry her. When in the end she agreed, it was partly because he was so unhappy, and partly because she saw that the great friendship between Ralph and Lytton might actually consolidate her own position."

It was Marshall herself who ended up falling in love with Ralph, as she recalled: "He was a tall, good-looking and very broad-shouldered man. His remarkably blue eyes never seemed quite still, conveyed an impression of great vitality held in check with difficulty, and often flashed in my direction, as I couldn't help observing."

At various moments during this time Strachey, Carrington and Partridge shared a farmhouse in Wiltshire, where Ralph would take Marshall during weekends, and where Marshall and Ralph would live after the deaths of Strachey and Carrington, until Ralph's own death.

Ralph had left Dora for Marshall before her suicide, and married Marshall afterwards. Marshall, too, had been drawn to Ralph because of his proximity to Strachey whom she loved. She and Ralph had a son they name Lytton Burgo Partridge. Both loved music, dancing, literature and debates, both were agnostic and pacifists, there was rarely a night they did not share the same bed, so in the end their marriage was more successful than most. Ralph Partridge died in 1960 at age 66 of a heart attack.

Frances Marshall Partridge lived to age 104 and is known for her diaries and the countless interviews she gave about her years in the Bloomsbury Set.

Their son Burgo died of a sudden heart attack at age 28, in 1962, three weeks after the birth of his daughter. He had married Henrietta Garnett, daughter of Angelica Garnett and David Garnett. He had been an author, most noted for his 1958 book *A History of Orgies* [which I've read and recommend].

As mentioned earlier, it was Roy Campbell who said that the Bloomsbury Set was a group of "sexless folk whose sexes intersect." Born in 1901 in Durban, Natal, South Africa, he grew up to adore horsemanship and hunting, as did all Natal boys, as well as a shared enthusiasm for alcohol. He also spoke Zulu fluently. He went to Oxford in 1918 but when he failed the entrance exams he turned to writing poetry, apparently inspired by both Nietzsche and Darwin. His entry into the Set had a major setback when his wife Mary fell in line with Bloomsbury promiscuity by falling in love with Vita Sackville-West, Virginia Woolf's sweetheart, bringing down the wrath of the highly influential Woolf on both of them. Campbell came to the conclusion that the Set was nothing more than a pack of immoral snobs, parasites that Campbell called "intellectuals without intellect". He made a clean break by taking his wife and two daughters to Toledo Spain where they converted to Catholicism, just as the Civil War was breaking out. It was in Toledo they witnessed the execution of 17 of the priests who had welcomed them, massacred in the streets by Communists, which turned Campbell into a supporter of Franco's Nationalists. He saw his family to safety in Marseille before returning to Spain as a war correspondent alongside Franco's armies. There was no sign of his becoming a Fascist, the death of his friends having been enough to turn him against the Republicans. During the Second World War he was posted to British East Africa, taking up residence afterwards in Oxford. He continued writing poetry and was considered the finest spiritual verse writer of his generation. In 1952 he and his family moved to Portugal where he translated French, Portuguese and Spanish poetry into English, as well as Spanish 16th and 17th century plays and the poetry of Federico García Lorca. He was killed in 1957 when his car left the road and smashed into a tree, his wife at the wheel.

One of Senhouse's loves was Michael Davies, 1900-1921, a poet of huge potential who died in what many believe was a suicide pact with his inseparable companion Rupert Buxton.

Michael and Rupert

Nico, one of the five Davies brothers, described Michael as "the cleverest of us, the most original, the potential genius."

Nico [Nicolas] Davies

J.M. Barrie, 1860-1937, wrote his *Peter Pan* based on Michael. Barrie had been a friend of the Davies family for several years, and was especially close to the Davies elder brother George. George and Michael were "the Ones" stated Nico, meaning Barrie's favorites. When the boys' parents died, their father in 1907, their mother in 1910, Barrie was appointed their guardian. George was killed on the W.W. I fields of Flanders in 1915.

Barrie was extremely small, 5' 3 ½". The defining period of his life seems to have been the loss of his brother, clearly his mother's favorite, who died in an ice-skating accident at age 13. Barrie did what he could to replace him to lighten his mother's pain, imitating his brother's voice and wearing his clothes.

A veracious reader, Barrie and his mother entertained each other with stories they invented. He went to a series of boarding schools from age 8 and after graduating from the University of Edinburgh he found work as a journalist. He published stories he and his mother had made up, and then turned to writing plays. Peter Pan originated as a play and then as a novel, *Peter and Wendy*.

Barrie kept up correspondence with an amazing number of people, Robert Louis Stevenson [his and his mother's favorite author], Shaw, H.G. Wells, Conan Doyle, Wodehouse, Kipling and the explorer Robert Falcon Scott. Barrie was the godfather of Scott's son Peter, and was one of the seven people Scott wrote to before his death during an expedition to the South Pole, requesting that he care for his son and wife.

Barrie himself married in 1894, a marriage universally reported an unconsummated and ended in divorce when his wife refused to remain faithful to him.

Barrie lived near the Davies family and was soon entertaining the boys with his stories and his ability to wiggle his ears. Peter Davies was the baby of the family at the time and Barrie assured the older boys that Peter had the ability to fly, something they were still young enough to believe. The boys' mother's will specified that she wanted Barrie to be their guardian, and to support the request Barrie claimed they had been engaged to marry. Although many believe Barrie was sexually involved with "the Ones", Nico Davies later wrote: "I don't believe Uncle Jim ever experienced what one might call 'a stirring in the undergrowth' for anyone--man, woman, or child. He was an innocent--which is why he could write Peter Pan."

Barrie suffered greatly after the loss of George and Michael. Before committing suicide in 1960 by throwing himself under a train, Peter Davies wrote *Morgue*, about Barrie and Peter's family. Barrie himself died of pneumonia in 1937, at age 77.

Michael as Peter Pan and his brother George Davies, "the Ones".

Michael went to Eton but hated being separated from "Uncle Jim" Barrie. He was nonetheless a brilliant student, especially in art and poetry, and deeply liked by his fellow students. He went up to Oxford where he met Rupert Buxton, a former student of Harrow [Cambridge, Oxford, Eton and Harrow are covered in my book *Boarding School Homosexuality*]. It was at both Eton and Oxford that Michael had an affair with Roger Senhouse, before he met Buxton.

A photo of Senhouse taken by his lover Lytton Strachey and a photo of Senhouse taken years after his love affair with Michael Davies [I'm deeply sorry for the poor quality of the pictures].

In a 1976 interview with Conservative politician Robert Boothby, Boothby stated: "I don't think Michael had any girlfriends, but our relationship was not homosexual. I believe it was--fleetingly--between him and Senhouse.''

John ''Jack'' Davies and Peter Davies, Peter age 13.

Days before Michael's 21st birthday he went swimming with Rupert Buxton in the Thames. A coroner's witness stated he saw the two boys swim out together and, forehead to forehead, they simply sank beneath the surface. One report stated their bodies were found ''clasped'' to each other, another ''tied together''. Michael's brothers Nico and Peter, and Barrie, all acknowledged that it was a suicide pact. The official record maintained that Michael, in difficulty, drowned accidently, as did Buxton while trying to save him.

The *Oxford Magazine* published this obituary: ''Two House men whose loss would have been more widely and more deeply mourned, it would be impossible to find. They were intimate friends, and in their death they were not divided. It is we who must learn to live without them''

THE POOL OF ILL-OMEN : TRAGEDY REPEATED AFTER 78 YEARS.

Sandford Pool, Oxford, where Mr. Michael Liewellyn Davies (inset) and Mr. Rupert Buxton, both undergraduates, were drowned while bathing. The bodies were recovered yesterday. Mr. Davies was one of Sir James Barrie's adopted sons; the other, believed to be the original of "Peter Pan," was killed in action. The monument in the picture commemorates two other Oxford men drowned there in 1843.

CHAPTER TWO

THE APOSTLES

THE CAMBRIDGE-FOUR SPY RING

The porosity between the Bloomsbury Set and the Apostles was total. Some Apostle members were also members of the Set, while Setters who were not card-carrying Apostles appreciated the intellectual contact of Apostle debates, and sexually both groups provided a recruitment center of boys, a chance to experience new ideas and philosophies while varying bodies and the infinite diversity of orgasms inherent in the exchanges, as nothing is more exciting than an unexplored mind, beautiful eyes that reflect one's own image, and the curiosity of uncovering layer after layer of clothing, warmer and warmer to the hand, the teeth and lips that envelope the last taut stretch of tissue, made tense by the hidden tumescence.

What is often inexplicable is how boys can be attracted to far older men, as was Marc Allégret to André Gide (1). Alan Sheridan, in his *André Gide*, asks the reasonable question, What did 15-year-old Marc Allégret see in 48-year-old André Gide. Certainly André awoke the boy intellectually and sexually, like Socrates "teaching his young lover how to use his body as well as his mind," writes Sheridan. In addition, early on in the relationship André had promised Marc that he would "initiate the young man into heterosexuality", continued Sheridan, as Marc was bisexual. Jean Cocteau also had access to Marc, Cocteau who attracted hordes of boys thanks to his contacts, charm and intelligence, boys who turned to Cocteau's handsome lover Jean Marais to fulfill their lust, but slept with Cocteau to advance their careers, to meet the right people, to have the best seats at the theater and opera and in restaurants. We have the example of heterosexual men who accept the affection of far older homosexuals, as Paul Roche did Duncan Grant, and the case of Daniel Guérin, a Marxist who helped working-class boys, who got to know them and they got to know and trust him, some of whom were willing to share a little romanticism, a little human warmth, and an ejaculation (1).

Today we have the example of heterosexual marines who shack up with homosexuals, as revealed in Scotty Bower's wonderful book *Full Service*. A Marine himself, Hollywood-based Scotty rented out his buddies to actors. His Marines often had a great time, were served great food around great pools, and did what his clients wanted, which was often just a human presence and a little mutual jerking off. Some of the boys wound up living with the men, for the reason found in the scene from *Some Like It Hot* where Jack Lemmon returns from his date with Osgood and declares to Tony Curtis that he and Osgood were going to get married. "Why would a guy marry another guy?" asked Curtis. "For *security*!" exclaims Lemmon.

Heterosexual boys have little difficulty in interacting with other heterosexual boys because they share the same body and bodily needs, the reason why Neapolitan lads state that their first sexual contact often takes place with transvestites, because of the anatomical similarities. Homosexual friendships in prep schools (2) are often extremely deep because they're a boy's first love, and due to the fact that these sexual liaisons last during many scholastic years, girls' bodies, when they are finally confronted with one, are as foreign as the discovery of another planet. Prep-school boys rarely find, with girls, the depth and totality of the sexual experiences they had with other boys, and their later marriages, sexually unsatisfying, take place largely for societal reasons and as a way of acquiring children, sons being a man's unique access to a form of immortality. Never ever will a prep-school lad forget the first boy he bedded, the first he "took", and the first he allowed to take him. Of course, the vast majority of English boys have not known the freedom of prep-school dormitories, where they could discover, among themselves, to what extent they were homosexual, heterosexual or omnisexual, unhindered by adults. It is these uninitiated boys who become queer bashers, who never experience the meaning of virile love, the intensity, the heat of mutual male give-and-take.

This then was the context of the exchanges between the Bloomsbury Set and the Apostles, along with the hundreds of boys on the periphery, those admitted to participate in the debates and take part in the plays the Apostles mounted, where they discovered, were they so inclined, the exceptional beauty of a Duncan Grant, a Rupert Brooke and a Michael Davies.

The Apostles is a Cambridge University discussion group founded in 1820, originally 12 in number, from which came the name. Meetings were held Saturday evenings, refreshments consisting of coffee and Whales, sardines on toast. New members are called embryos, becoming, later, angels. The group's papers and books were kept in a cedar chest they dubbed the Ark. Eleven of the original 12 were buried in the same cemetery, proof of the group's cohesion until death.

Some of the subjects of debate were "Is self abuse bad as an end?" [most voting No!] and one debate was entitled, "Achilles or Patroclus," supposedly meaning lust against friendship (3). As stated, many members of the Apostles were also part of the Bloomsbury Set.

One of the first embryos, Frederick Maurice, encouraged members to give up their inner thoughts, confessions that were analyzed and debated, the antithesis of what went on during the times when free thought was stifled because it was considered embarrassing and too personal. Soul-searching introspection was eased by drugs such as opium, and members were encouraged to experiment in this and other domains.

Two Apostles who did not hide their homosexuality were Alfred Tennyson and Arthur Hallam, homosexuality which, added to Apostle interest in psychology, experimentation in drugs and other liberalities, became the founding cement that ultimately was responsible for the Apostles' success in gaining a larger membership as well as becoming increasingly secret to cover up Society "research". As Richard Deacon in his *The Cambridge Apostles* writes, love between members was "the beginning of a kind of sublimated homosexual cult within the Society." Of the Tennyson/Hallam couple another member, Frances Brookfield, declared "our minds are dazzled by the Apostles' achievements, and our hearts are warmed by their mutual love."

Hallam died only four years after being elected an Apostle and Tennyson wrote,

> "Forgive my grief for one removed,
> The creature whom I found so fair."

Tennyson and the fair Hallam. Called *le jeune homme fatal* thanks to his beauty, Hallam (1811-1833) went from Eton to Trinity College Cambridge and into the Apostles where as an 18-year-old he slept with Tennyson, 20, and proposed marriage to Tennyson's sister, par for the course in those times as described in the An Overview chapter on the Bloomsbury Set. On holiday in Vienna he caught a chill and the resulting fever carried him off in his sleep at age 22.

Apostle boys were ''eager to savour new experiences and explore new horizons,''' wrote Deacon. John Sterling, a member, wrote, ''Commend me to the brethren, who, I trust, are waxing daily in religion and radicalism.... To my education in that Society I feel I owe every power I possess.... From the Apostles I, at least, learned to think as a free man.''

The discovery of sex that went on in all boarding schools was just that: the occasion for boys to explore their bodies and the immense pleasure they could offer each other. Some went on to become heterosexual, some homosexual, most omnisexual, as said, but in all cases the mystic discovery of first love would remain an integral part of them until death. Most of the boys fathered sons of their own, boys for whom they had great sexual tolerance thanks to the countless nights when the men themselves had experienced first bliss, first love and first pain, beside, and often inside, one of their own.

Those with particularly developed homosexual affinities found a welcome compost in the Apostles, and as Apostle members opened their ranks to boys known for their homosexual preferences, the ranks of those who practiced what they called Socratic love. Like today's gays who flock to Hollywood, San Francisco and Miami thanks to the affable climate, so too did word get out that the Apostles was the place to be for boys who did boys. The emotional experiences of boyish exploration became, as they aged, love between youths and, later, when youths became adults, they turned their attention to boys. Apostles who had started out as students became schoolmasters, predators of lads just immerging from puberty.

William Johnson Cory, for example, an Apostle who was characterized as "the most brilliant Eton tutor of his day," loved by his students who called him Tute [for tutor], "the wisest master who has ever been to Eton," stated a colleague. He wrote a justification for learning Latin, stating that it "enforced the habit of attention ... assuming at a moment's notice a new intellectual position ... entering quickly into another's intellectual thoughts ... [encouraging] minute points of accuracy ... and mental soberness."

He penned a book of poems, *Ionica*, dedicated to pretty-faced Charles Wood, that laid "down the principle that affection between people of the same sex is no less natural and irrational than the ordinary passionate relations."

After 27 years at Eton he was forced to retire due to improper conduct with boys, of whom Eton was a limitless source.

Oscar Browning was partially known for his feud with Virginia Woolf who accused him of not only thinking that "the best woman was intellectually inferior to the worst man," but she outed his preference for boys. Browning was educated at Eton, a student of William Johnson Cory. He went on to King's College, Cambridge, where he became a fellow and a member of the Apostles.

He, too, was dismissed from Eton as a result of a homosexual scandal there, in 1875. He went on to teach at Cambridge and founded a training college for teachers. He was also president of the Cambridge Footlights. His nephew and biographer purportedly destroyed his diaries and letters as protection against further scandal concerning his involvement with young men. [Only thanks to diaries that have survived do we know a little about the sex lives of Roger Casement, Maynard Keynes and a few others.] In love with Italy like so many before him, Browning died in Rome in 1923.

Boys who went to Cambridge were the chosen few, those who had inherited the earth, and they knew it. Charles Merivale, later Dean of Ely, was an Apostle who stated that Apostles were comfortable among themselves because they had common intellectual tastes and aspirations, mutually flattering each other, mutually conceited, and that it was up to them to enlighten the rest of the world: "We lived in constant intercourse with one another, day by day, met over our wine and our tobacco." To this Richard Deacon adds: "It was in such intercourse in the rooms of individual members of the Society that homosexuality flourished."

As I wrote in my book *Boarding School Homosexuality*, most of these lads went on to marry, as did Oscar Wilde, but the marriages were rarely sexually fulfilling, as the memory of the emotions and lust of first love can never be excelled.

The underlying fact that men faced prison for their acts only reinforced the luck they had to find themselves in the protected walls of the Apostles, where imprisonment *à la* Oscar Wilde was an impossibility. Godsworthy Lowes Dickinson, an Apostle, suggested also that homosexuals escaped public wrath because people, like the Queensberrys, did not suspect that sex was going on simply because two men lived together.

It was Goldsworthy who initiated the idea of the League of Nations. Called Goldie, he was in love with Roger Frey whom we meet in the Bloomsbury Set, perhaps platonically as Fry preferred to be known more for his heterosexuality than his homosexuality, and Dickinson's philosophy was based on Neo-Platonism [although nearly all claimed virginal Platonism, before and after joint orgasms].

Goldie entered the boarding school of Beomonds, then Charterhouse School, from ages 14 to 19, followed by King's College, Cambridge. In 1896 he wrote *The Greek View of Life*. E.M. Forster wrote the biography of Dickinson after Dickinson's death in 1932 but omitted all information concerning Dickinson's homosexuality and foot fetishism. Dickinson wrote dozens of books, one of which was *The Magic Flute: A Fantasia to Plato and his Dialogues*. His relationships with young men were both sexual and fatherly, certainly an ideal figure for a boy needing warm guidance from a man who would show him the way, instructing him intellectually while satisfying him tenderly and physically, yet without the virile dimension so vital in Ancient Greece [for the simple reason that most dons were uptight swishy pansies].

Dickinson was reputed as having been remarkably candid in exposing Platonic homoerotism by stating, "that there was another side to the matter goes without saying. This passion, like any other, has its depths, as well as its heights." Daring for the times, apparently.

The expression Higher Sodomy was now invented. In the Bloomsbury Set it was defined as meaning a Platonic approach to homosexuality, while in the Apostles it apparently also meant Higher in the sense that love between men was infinitely more valorizing than that between men and women. In fact, there was nothing Platonic about their relations: these men were fucking each other, called Lower Sodomy.

Julian Bell was an Apostle whose parents and their Feydeauesque lives is covered in the Bloomsbury Set, An Overview, and in Duncan Grant's chapter. The philosopher G.E. Moore's sexuality is hard to discern, although philosophically he went from a passionate believer in God to a man who gave up his faith, stating that one "should spread skepticism until at last everyone knows we can know absolutely nothing." Homosexuality became a "must" in the Apostles and the Bloomsbury Set, to the extent that Duncan Grant said "even the womanizers pretend to be sods, lest they shouldn't be thought respectable."

Frederic William Henry Myers, 1843-1901, was a devoted--meaning highly randy--Apostle homosexual, two of whose bed companions were J.A. Symonds and Henry Sidgwick. Later in life he was said to have been as enthusiastically heterosexual as homosexual [one of his maidens committed suicide in the tradition of Dora Carrington]. He seems to have replaced religion with psychical research, spending the rest of his life with mediums, spiritualists, the paranormal and telepathy, and was said to have swallowed any charlatan tomfoolery that came his way. He also used his psychical research as a means of fulfilling his need for voyeuristic sex, thanks to his deep delving into the intimate aspects of his subjects' lives.

Henry Sidgwick, philosopher and economist, 1838-1900, founded the Society of Psychical Research with his lover Myers and others. An agnostic--as were many Apostles at some time in their lives, although an amazing number seem to have converted to Catholicism near the end--he had difficulty coming to terms with his homosexuality, as did Symonds, which may in part have led to his marrying. Historian Piers Paul Read had spoken with some Apostles. He wrote that when "I mentioned Plato, Kant, Nietzsche, Marx or Sartre, I was treated with a pained smile, or a scoffing laugh ... such speculative, continental fun-philosophies were considered quite outside the bounds of serious study." The Apostles obviously considered themselves brilliant, yet their bumbling approach to sexuality--from the extreme of publicly humping each other in dormitories to the lows of submitting to highly unfulfilling marriages--leaves me perplex at their inability to confront something as mundane as sex, and this despite their belief in their own stellar genius. Added to this was the silliness of the séances men like Sidgwick attended, as far afield as Paris and Naples.

Sidgwick

Roden Noel, 1834-1894, was enamored of his own body: ''I was immensely vain of my physical beauty,'' and he claimed that the homosexual part of his bisexuality was inherited from his great uncle, Percy Jocelyn, forced to flee London when found in the arms of a soldier. His first sexual memory as a little boy was being caressed by his father's footman. He was also said to have been the first to have fucked J.A. Symonds. Selected extracts from his works include: ''eyes dim-dewy with desire'', ''appleblooming boys'', ''bronze harvestmen'', ''his back so tender''. As with Proust who disguised his boys as women in order for his *oeuvre* to be published (11), one can only wonder at what marvels men like Noel, Byron, and others could have come up with had laws and society allowed freedom of artistic expression, and had Proust had the balls to tell the truth.

Noel by George Richmond.

The ubiquitous Lytton Strachey was responsible for the Ark, the trunk in which the Apostles kept their secret papers, and used its private content to unmask Apostle homosexual members, which aided his search for young prey. Strachey compensated for his homeliness by developing a cunning, Machiavelli presence that, combined with manipulative genius, brought him to the center of Apostle power, a man one had to content sexually if one wished entry into the Apostles, a dictator whose impact influenced countless books written at the time. Strachey worked in tandem with Maynard Keynes, both who raised the love of boys to a veritable godly level [didn't Zeus have his Ganymede and Apollo his Hyacinth (4), as well as James I his George? (3)]. When Keynes went on to marry, the shock of his treason equaled that of Burgess's, stated one Apostle. Both Keynes and Strachey vetted new embryos, and beauty replaced the criteria of brains, although an aristocratic background continued to have importance, albeit well behind sexual promise. Arthur Hobhouse, for example was chosen and immediately seduced by Keynes, Keynes who signed his letters to Hobhouse ''Your constant true love, JMK''. [Both Strachey and Keynes have individual chapters in this book.]

The appeal of the Society must have been an enormous magnet for boys looking for other handsome boys, thanks to Strachey and Keynes's selections, and the Apostles became ever-more secret because, as Strachey wrote Keynes, people in general, and "dowagers" in particular, would never accept the image of boys inserting their dicks in the asses of other boys, my choice of words for Strachey's more refined comment that "the best among the Apostles were sodomitical."

A change apparently took place after the Strachey/Keynes tandem with the election of the homosexual Ludwig Wittgenstein who wanted the Apostles known for other things than a homosexual harem, especially when he had to keep his own favorites from the roving hands of Apostle members.

Wittgenstein

Bertrand Russell taught Ludwig Wittgenstein at Cambridge and found him "the most perfect example I have ever known of genius as traditionally conceived; passionate, profound, intense." Born in Vienna into a *richissime* family [Brahms and Mahler regularly gave concerts in their homes], their extreme wealth did not keep three of his brothers from committing suicide. His *Philosophical Investigations*, studies in the philosophy of mathematics, of the mind and of language, was published after his death. The family, formerly Jews, were baptized Catholics and Wittgenstein was deeply devoted to Christianity before becoming agnostic. Wittgenstein never forgot his Jewish heritage and blamed it for his imperfection, saying that "even the greatest Jewish thinker is no more than talented, myself for instance". He was in the same school and class as Hitler, but then Hitler was held back a grade and Wittgenstein advanced a grade, so they may not have met. Had Russell been homosexual he would have taken Wittgenstein as a lover, stating, "I love him. He is *the* young man one hopes for." Wittgenstein's three known lovers were David Pinsent, Francis Skinner and Ben Richards.

Pinset and Wittgenstein/Richards and Wittgenstein.
Wittgenstein joined the Austro-Hungarian Army in W.W. I fighting the British. His repeated bravery won him innumerable medals. Physically and mentally spent after the war, he became an elementary and then a primary school teacher and a monastery gardener, a multi-millionaire who lived in one room with bed and washstand, his meals consisting, according to a visitor, of coarse bread, butter and cocoa. Back at Cambridge Wittgenstein wrote his thesis for a PhD that philosophers Russell and Moore were given to read, Wittgenstein telling them, ''Don't worry. I know you'll never understand it.'' Wittgenstein wasn't arrogant so much as he simply believed in his absolute superiority. When he went to Cambridge Keynes remarked, ''Well, God has arrived. I met him on the 5.15 train.'' In fact, Wittgenstein took over Moore's chair in philosophy, after which he became a British citizen. When his former lover Francis Skinner died in 1941 Wittgenstein took up with Skinner's teenage friend Keith Kirk. He died simply stating ''I've had a wonderful life.'' [The Wikipedia article on Wittgenstein is of extraordinary brilliance.]

Deacon points out that whereas being called ''my dear boy'' in Strachey/Keynes times was a coveted compliment, after Wittgenstein it became a slap in the face, illustrated by an Apostle angel, Sir John Sheppard, who referred to a fellow Apostle as ''my very own precious boy,'' getting, in response, this admonition: ''I am not a boy, I am not precious and I am in no way whatsoever yours or anyone else's boy.'' Unheard of until then.

Sexual exploits in the Apostles became more muted, although Deacon does refer to an Apostle dinner that took place later, in 1937, after which the boys retired to the home of Eddie Marsh for an all-night orgy. This reveals a great deal about what had been going on throughout the years, but Deacon mentioned it as a bacchanalia that marked the end of an era, meaning that sexual hijinks went on, but more muzzled.

**Eddie Marsh standing behind Winston Churchill, 1907.
Marsh was Churchill's private secretary for 21 years, and was knighted
upon retirement. He was an influent Apostle and collected works of art
produced by the Bloomsbury Set, with whom he was intimately involved.**

The Cambridge-Four Spy Ring

When Donald Maclean was suspected of espionage in 1951 his Soviet handler, Yuri Modin, convinced Guy Burgess to flee at the same time. Many historians believe that Modin had promised Burgess that he could return to London, and indeed, after the news of the duo's espionage had become public, Burgess had asked a British delegation visiting Moscow to arrange things so that he could go back to England, at least long enough to be at his dying mother's side. The British Attorney General told then-Prime Minister Macmillan [whose brother Daniel was had been Keynes's lover] that there was not enough proof against Burgess to bring him to trial, and that there was perhaps not enough even against Maclean. But they were given false information which led both spies to believe the contrary, so that Burgess's mother died without seeing her son again and Maclean, apparently planning to defect back to England from Cuba where he was on visit, decided against it. In the end Burgess's ashes were buried very discreetly beside the body of his mother in Hampshire after Burgess's death in 1963 at age 52, death resulting from a life of alcoholism and extreme stress due to his espionage.

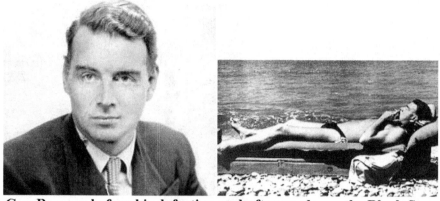

Guy Burgess before his defection and afterwards, on the Black Sea.

Guy Francis de Moncy Burgess betrayed his country for philosophical reasons, not for money as his family, former French Huguenots [the name Burgess comes from Bourgeois], had been bankers and his father a naval officer. His homosexuality found its Nirvana at Eton and Cambridge, where he was a member of the largely homosexual Cambridge Apostles.

Burgess, Donald Maclean, Anthony Blunt and Kim Philby formed the Cambridge-Four Spy Ring, of which Burgess and Blunt were homosexual and Maclean bisexual, their preference being for boys, not sex between themselves, even if they had at times lived together during their careers.

Blunt, Maclean, Burgess and Philby

Burgess's own career saw him working in propaganda at MI6 and as a producer of the BBC program *The Week in Westminster*, which covered Parliamentary activity and brought him a great deal of information over informal teas, immediately passed on to the KGB. But it was as an assistant to the Minister of State in the Foreign Office that he was given access to Top Secret documents that he passed to his controller at night to be photographed, and that he put back in the Minister's cabinets before dawn.

For a time Burgess lived with Philby, despite the fact that Philby's wife remembered what had taken place when they were stationed in Istanbul where Burgess's residence was full of drunkenness and homosexual orgies. The presence of Burgess put a huge strain on her marriage with Philby.

A fight with a member of the Royal Automobile Club saw Burgess lose his balance and fall down a flight of marble steps, suffering skull fractures from which he never fully recovered, and which obliged him to frequent sanitariums on the Black Sea. He hated Russian life, their refusal to accept homosexuality, even if he was permitted a live-in boyfriend. He never learned Russian and his suits and liquor were imported from London.

Incredibly, Kim Philby had been in line to take command of MI6 and blamed his downfall on "that bloody man Burgess", when attention turned to him following the headlines of Burgess's betrayal.

On the day Burgess fled, his lover Jack "Jacky" Hewit wrote that Guy was in bed "reading a book and smoking, and he seemed normal and unworried. When I left the flat to go to my office, Guy said 'See you later, Mop'--that was his pet name for me. We intended to have a drink together that evening." Mop did the cooking and looked after their home. An off-and-on lover, Mop had originally been a dancer in his youth. That morning Maclean had gone to his office too, but his colleagues had made sure he would handle nothing of political value because they had become increasingly suspicious of him. Maclean was 38, and it was his birthday. Burgess was 40.

Christopher Isherwood cruised the wartime blacked-out beaches of Californian, and Burgess did the same during London blackouts, picking up young servicemen. He would arrive at his office after a night of screwing and pass around half-naked photos of a recent conquest, doing nothing to hide his taste for boys. He was said to have been boorish, a chain smoker and always had a bottle of gin in his desk, a desk in a perpetual mess, with even secret documents strewn over the surface. One of the reasons he was tolerated was that he would agree to work Saturday afternoons, which everyone else wanted off, the occasion to rifle through the files he would hand over to his handler. The Soviets said that he was extremely adept at hunting out secrets, like a dog did truffles. He met his handler, Modin, daily. Modin later said, "His reports were thoughtful and clear. He took no notes because his memory was faultless." Despite giving Burgess a great deal of money, enough even to buy a secondhand Rolls-Royce, Modin claimed that Burgess worked for ideological reasons only. Apparently the one thing he refused the Soviets was their request that he marry in order to better cover up his espionage, something he couldn't go through with physically.

Burgess liked his sex rough and dirty, and was said to have had a huge member, "gargantuan" said one, "a whopper" another. "It had to be seen to be believed," recounted a boyfriend, "the secret weapon of his charm."

Burgess

In 1963 Philby fled to Russia where he experienced the second greatest deception of his life with the Soviets, the first being the Molotov-Ribbentrop Pact that divided Poland between Germany and Russia: the downfall of the Soviet system where the old were treated like so much garbage--"After all," he wrote, "they [soldiers now old] won the war". He had believed in the ideal of communism to the extreme extent of betraying those he himself, when he worked for the British, had sent to their deaths: "They knew the risks they were running. I was serving the interests of the Soviet Union and those interests required that those men were defeated. To the extent that I helped defeat then, even if it caused their deaths, I have no regrets." But he certainly had regrets for himself. Pensioned off at 500 rubles a month, allowed to visit the KGB for the first time *ten years* after his arrival in Moscow, he lost himself in alcohol and depression, and tried to kill himself some time during the 1960s. Only when he died in 1988, at age 76, did the USSR honor him with a very public hero's funeral.

Philby said it perfectly: "The ideals were right but the way they were carried out was wrong. The fault lay with the people in charge."

Philby was nearly tripped up a dozen times. In 1938 the Russian Krivitsky defected to the United States and warned that there were two spies in the British Foreign Office [Burgess and Maclean], as well as a British journalist covering the Spanish Civil War, the job Philby held at that moment. Krivitsky was shot dead in his Washington hotel room. Philby had gone to Spain to assassinate Franco, a plan abandoned by the Soviets when they found Philby willing to sacrifice himself, but possessing neither the physical courage nor the "other qualities necessary for the attempt," wrote his Soviet handler.

Philby's Soviet controller in Madrid defected, intimately aware of each of Philby's treasonous activities. Stalin got word to him that his family in Russia would survive so long as Philby's identity remained secret.

James Jesus Angleton met with Philby and suspected him of being the "third man", and this both before Angleton became director of the CIA and afterwards, but his doubts were apparently never taken seriously.

In 1945 Konstantin Volkov, vice-consul of Istanbul, defected, for money, promising to give up three British spies, two in the Foreign Office and one working in counter-espionage in London, Philby's job at that time. Philby himself was given the task of dealing with Volkov who was kidnapped before he could board a British plane leaving Istanbul and was shipped back to Moscow wrapped in bandages [an incident later used in several spy movies and books].

More incredible still, Philby's ability to get out of hot spots was such that in Moscow some people believed he was a double-agent, working in reality for the British. Philby told Moscow that there were *no* double-agents working for the English government and that the British government was certain no double-agents from other countries had infiltrated the British government, nor were there any spies on British territory, eliciting the unbelieving response from Moscow, "Could the British Intelligence Service be such fools they failed to notice suitcase-loads of paper leaving the office?" Added to this was the fact that Philby's first wife had been a communist, as had Philby in his younger days, causing Moscow to ask: "Could they have overlooked Philby's communist wife?" [to which they could have added, but didn't, "And Philby's belonging to the communist party too?"].

Philby's life was the grist of several Le Carré books, and only a Le Carré can successfully exploit the convoluted twists and turns of an existence like Philby's. But in ways Philby's life was secondary to another man of adventure, Philby's own father. St John Philby had been an author, orientalist and a convert to Islam. He had been an Indian Civil Servant and an advisor to the King of Saudi Arabia, Ibn Sa'ud. He had named his son Kim from Kipling's novel, although Kim Philby's full name was Harold Adrian Russell Philby. He took his son to Saudi Arabia in his teens and placed him with Bedouins "to be turned into a man" [alas, we don't know exactly what he meant by this]. Later Kim was sent to Westminster School and then to Cambridge.

I'm not going to enumerate all the posts he held and the women he married, but one striking point was the number of Soviet handlers sent to retrieve his material, most of whom eventually received a bullet in the back of the head on their return to Russia, due to Stalin's Great Purge.

It was Philby who became aware that Maclean had been tripped up when a Soviet cipher clerk inadvertently used a one-time pad *twice*, which allowed the second message, implicating Maclean, to be decoded. Philby sent Burgess a message telling him to get Maclean out of Britain, in coached terms: "The Lincoln convertible you left in the parking lot has to be removed immediately or it will be too late ... it will be sent to the scrap heap.''

But Philby had warned Burgess not to escape with Maclean, stating ''Don't go with him when he goes. If you do, that'll be the end of me. Swear that you won't.'' He later claimed that Burgess, ''that bloody man'', had destroyed him by fleeing, as reported.

The scandal of the departure of Burgess and Maclean finally awoke MI6 to the multiple rumors concerning Philby, who underwent interrogation--''I have never been a communist!'', he maintained throughout--and was not only let off, but Harold Macmillan went before the House of Commons and declared, ''I have no reason to conclude that Mr. Philby has at any time betrayed the interests of his country, or to identify him with the so-called 'third man', if indeed there was one.''

Philby nonetheless left MI6 and in 1956 went to Beirut as a reporter for *The Observer* and *The Economist*. In England in '57 his wife was found dead from a deliberate overdose, although Philby was declared her murderer by some because she knew too much. In '59 he remarried [no question of homosexuality here] to a woman who later described his bouts with deep depression and alcoholism. He was confronted by a friend who had figured out his treason: ''I once looked up to you, Kim. My God, how I despise you now.'' Philby admitted all and when the friend asked for a signed confession, Philby told him to return when he [Philby] had sobered up. Soon afterwards a cargo ship left Beirut in such a hurry its cargo was left scattered on the docks, although other reports had him leave overland by way of Syria.

Blunt's destiny was certainly not espionage, and he only fell into it because, as he said, in the '30s every thinking intellectual was a Marxist, in the same way that it was chic to be homosexual and be part of the Cambridge Apostles, of which one was often both. ''I was so naive politically that I was not justified in committing myself to any political action. The atmosphere at Cambridge was so intense, the enthusiasm for any anti-fascist activity was so great, that I made the biggest mistake of my life.'' His Soviet controller agreed, calling Blunt ''an ideological shit''. The Soviets nonetheless wanted him to defect along with Burgess and Maclean, but Blunt refused any thought of leaving civilization for the rough conditions existent in Russia.

He therefore agreed to tell all in 1964 in exchange for immunity and the promise that his treason would be kept a secret for 15 years, which was the case when, in 1979, Thatcher outed him. The incredible publicity forced him into monk-like seclusion until his death at age 75 in 1983.

Anthony Frederick Blunt had been an expert in art and was said to have written the never-equaled *Art and Architecture in France 1500-1700* and an equally never-equaled study on Poussin. After spending his childhood in Paris he went on through the usual homosexuality at Marlborough College and then on to Trinity College, Cambridge, on a *mathematics* scholarship, Cambridge where he later taught French. He was recruited by the Soviets after a visit to the Soviet Union. When he spilled the beans in 1964 he didn't hesitate to name the boys/men he had recruited. During the war his treason amounted to telling the Soviets what the Germans were up to, and later he passed on so much information to Russia that the Soviets, as they did with Burgess, suspected him of being a double-agent, stating that the English could not be so stupid as to be unaware that Blunt was giving up so many files. One of his legitimate assignments during the war was to retrieve the compromising letters the Duke of Windsor had written to Hitler, located in the Schloss Friedrichshof in Germany, letters now in the Royal Archives.

Donald Duart Maclean read modern languages at Trinity Hall, Cambridge, where he played rigby and joined the Communist Party, declaring later that he wasn't a Marxist and had become a party member through an *erreur de jeunesse*. When he applied for diplomatic service he was interrogated: "By the way, Mr Maclean. We understand that you, like other young men, held strong Communist views while you were at Cambridge. Do you still hold those views?" He replied: "I did have such views--and I haven't entirely shaken them off." Maclean later recalled: "I think they must have liked my honesty because they nodded, looked at each other and smiled." Maclean was accepted.

He was recruited by the Soviets in 1934 and passed his Civil Service Examination with ''first class honors'' the same year. He started work in the Foreign Office in '35 and became Third Secretary at the British Embassy in Paris in '38. He married in '39. In '48 he became head of Chancery at the British embassy in Cairo. His wife had an affair with an Egyptian aristocrat, while Maclean's work was increasingly questioned by both the British and Americans due to the decryption of certain coded messages suggesting he was a spy, again because of one-time coded message pads that had been re-used. The Soviets were eager to have him in Moscow because he was considered the weakest link in their espionage chain, a man who would easily crack, as had Blunt.

Once in Russia he seemed to have been like a fish in water. Joined by his wife whom he had forgiven for her infidelity [while he himself had never stopped having homosexual encounters, which had put a strain on his marriage]. He learned Russian and earned a doctorate. Before leaving Britain for Moscow his wife had declared: ''I will not admit that my husband, the father of my children, is a traitor to his country.'' She then lapsed into silence, which continued to her death. Back in Moscow she became Philby's lover, Philby who divorced his wife in order to marry her, which put an end to Philby and Maclean's friendship. She tired of Philby after three years and returned to Maclean, with whom she remained until his death in 1983 at age 69 [who would believe this, even in a Le Carré novel?]. Maclean's ashes were returned to Britain and scattered over his parents' graves.

CHAPTER THREE

DAVID [BUNNY] GARNETT

At age 22 David Garnett was described by a friend, Michael Fordham, as ''very beautiful and seemed to me like a god''. Garnett was universally called Bunny because of the gift of a rabbit-skin cloak offered him as a child, but I will not use the moniker for someone so central to the history of the Bloomsbury Set. It was during a weeklong hiking trek that he came upon Duncan Grant at a cottage called ''The Lacket''. Duncan had apparently seen him for the first time two years previously and had fallen in love with David then. Several months later David and Duncan met at a party hosted by Maynard Keynes. Duncan declared himself to David and persuaded him to return to his home where David was given the bed while Duncan slept on the floor, David's hand, which he refused to relinquish, his only consolation. Duncan wrote David, telling him how ''*miserable*'' he was without him, underlying the word in his letter. They met again in January 1913, David now 21, Duncan 28, at another party. They returned home together and this time David gave himself fully to Duncan. David wrote in his journal that he [David] had felt a passion ''borne partly of curiosity about this darling strange creature so like an animal & so full of charm''. And indeed Duncan was of exquisite beauty, warm, wonderfully teasing, the incarnation of charisma. David was supremely lucky.

David Garnett by Duncan Grant.

Of course, David had been broken in sexually in prep schools, and it was now that he may have realized to what extent he was omnisexual, although, he insisted throughout his life, he was basically heterosexual. He knew that Duncan was homosexual, experienced enough to fulfill David's sexual needs. David was far from the first person Duncan claimed he could not live without, and whose absence made him miserable, words whose purpose, in the mouths of most men, was to ''score'' and move on. But they were uttered sincerely by Duncan, in this case at least, as his past sex had been fleeting couplings with Maynard Keynes, Adrian Stephen, Lytton Strachey and numerous others. David, now in safe hands, had physically entered that most beautiful segment of his life [enjoyed by so many boys in their teens and early twenties], when people couldn't get enough of looking at him. He took full advantage of the fact, never missing a chance to conclude sexually, a preference for threesomes with a girl and another boy, the girl whom he would at times later meet alone, declaring to one [as he confided to his journal], ''I never want to see a man again & speak to one. How sick I am of all this dull sodomitical twaddle.'' David had especially been offended by Lytton Strachey who had turned to David as they were walking down a busy London street and kissed him hard on the mouth, causing David to rush off in the nearest taxi.

As stated above, Duncan had a fleeting affair with Adrian Stephen, who was Vanessa Bell's younger brother, meaning that Duncan was having sex with Adrian at perhaps the very same moment he was impregnating Vanessa, the mother of Duncan's future child [the affair with Adrian was far too fleeting for Duncan who was genuinely in love with him]. In fact, it was Adrian who had introduced Duncan to his sister Vanessa. Adrian would later become one of England's first psychoanalysts. It was thanks to his sister's having bought a home in Bloomsbury where she establish her salon that Adrian found himself in the middle of the Bloomsbury Set and the unlimited sex, male and female, it provided him. [Although, his biographer maintains that it was Adrian the true founder of the Bloomsbury Set.] Adrian became the editor of the *International Journal of Psychoanalysis*, a position held until then by none other than Lytton Strachey's brother James. There was another brother in the Stephen family, Toby, who, along with Adrian, had been two of Lytton Strachey's conquests. He died at age 26, of typhoid, in Greece. Adrian died at age 65.

Adrian by Duncan.

Before momentarily leaving Adrian Stephen, perhaps the reader would allow me to recall two events that made Adrian immortal at the time, and brought the Bloomsbury Set to the public's attention. The first was the Cambridge Hoax of 1905. The Sultan of Zanzibar was visiting England and Adrian telegraphed the mayor of Cambridge, asking him to receive the Sultan with all due honors, which was done at the railway station where the mayor met Adrian and four of his pals in blackface, dressed in robs and wearing turbans. The charade was a success and when the boys notified the *Daily Mail* all hell broke out. Despite the mayor's demands, the chancellor of Cambridge University refused to expulse the lads in order to not throw fuel on the damage already done by the mayor himself.

The boys' next exploit made even more papers, including those abroad. Adrian and his pals sent a telegram to the HMS *Dreadnought* moored at Dorset. This time Duncan Grant was part of the gang, already Adrian's lover, Grant age 25, Adrian 27. They were now Abyssinians, their skin darkened and again in robes and turbans. A VIP coach was sent to Paddington Station in London to bring them to the ship where they were welcomed with flags and music. Speaking a hodgepodge of Latin and Greek, the lads demanded prayer mats and bestowed honors on the ship's officers. Afterwards the *Daily Mirror* was notified and the boys' arrest was ordered, but it turned out they'd broken no laws then in vigor. During the boys' visit to the *Dreadnought* they had consistently used the words Banga Banga. Later, when the *Dreadnought* rammed and sank a German submarine, the only ship to ever do so, the commander of the *Dreadnought* received a telegram of felicitations, signed BANGA, BANGA! [A story wonderfully recounted in Wikipedia.]

Vanessa Bell was in love with Duncan, which didn't stop her from trying to bed David, whom David found still beautiful at age 36, 13 years older than he. A woman who was inherently decent, she offered her country farmhouse to David and Duncan, David writing in his journal that the two men spent the time sunning themselves and in "the sweet lassitude of sleeping in each other's arms".

David had a school friend, his best friend, Frankie [Francis] Birrell, with whom he had found it natural to experiment sexually when young. David would always be the love of Frankie's life, Frankie telling him as early as 1915 "I show no signs of falling in love with anybody else". Both were invited to D.H. Lawrence's home for a weekend, Lawrence who had known David for some time and found him changed by the evil influence of the Bloomsbury Set, wondering if the boy had taken the path of Duncan Grant and Maynard Keynes. Lawrence, in his journal, admitted to being attracted to David, which disturbed him because he in no way wanted to succumb to homosexuality, an unnecessary diversion. Lawrence wrote this letter to David, brought to us by Sarah Knights in her wonderful *A Life of David Garnett*: "It is foolish of you to say that it doesn't matter either way-- the men loving men. It doesn't matter in the public way. But it matters so much, David, to the man himself that it is a blow of triumphant decay, when I meet Birrell or the others. I simply can't bear it. Why is there this horrible sense of frowstiness, so repulsive, as if it came from deep inward dirt--a sort of sewer--deep in men like K [eynes] and B [irrell] and D [uncan] G [rant]." David never saw Lawrence again. [If a man as intelligent as Lawrence could hold such opinions, it's easy to understand the disgust of the largely uneducated public--then as today.]

Always a good sport, Vanessa Bell wrote Roger Fry stating she felt "happier about Duncan and Bunny because I see that Bunny really does care a good deal for him."

But Duncan's jealousy got the best of their friendship, especially as David was sleeping around, something Duncan suspected, and then he once came on David, drunk, who was kissing Keynes [Keynes never refused an occasion to conclude with a boy, but he had nothing of Strachey's aggressiveness in doing so--he'd never stoop to stealing a kiss on a public street]. In addition, David met a girl, apparently a prostitute, who introduced him to cocaine and very knowledgeable sex, sex they would occasional have in Duncan's studio. Provocation or not, it drove Duncan up the walls. [Strangely, Duncan told David that he could sleep with all the boys he wanted, that only his sleeping with girls made him jealous, strange to my eyes because it's the opposite of what I personally feel--girls are okay, other boys not.]

Duncan and David were separated by some voluntary humanitarian aid David wanted to perform in France, accompanied by Frankie, but he returned in 1915 to a royal welcome by the Bloomsbury Set, notably Strachey who had never stopped writing him, Vanessa Bell, Keynes and of course Duncan, whom David had hugely missed during his months away, and for all his insistence on being heterosexual, it was a period in his life when, basically, only males counted.

Conscription became obligatory in January 1916 and all of the Bloomsbury Set applied to work as conscientious objectors, Duncan, Clive Bell, James and Lytton Strachey, Keynes, Garnett, all except Ralph Partridge. Rupert Brooke enlisted, as did Partridge, but Brooke lost his life.

Keynes persuaded both David and Duncan that the best way to remain outside of combat, to assure their continuation as conscientious objectors and to help their country, was to become farmers, which both men did, in the village of Wissett. For a while David was on his own while Duncan was ill in London, during which time David wrote to his lover, telling him outright of his need for women, even providing the names of those he was then bedding. Duncan finally got to Wissett, accompanied by Vanessa's children Julian and Quentin. Soon Wissett became a second home for the Bloomsbury Set, and even Vanessa's husband Clive Bell showed up with one of his mistresses. Strachey dropped by, still bent on getting more from David than a fleeting kiss in the middle of a busy street [although Strachey, in his journal, suggested that he had already copulated with David, and that he was at Wissett in the hope of doing so again "under Duncan's nose", he wrote. Bloomsbury at its purest]. Virginia and Leonard Woolf dropped by, David squeezing himself between them in one of the farmhouse beds [he wrote in his journal without providing further details]. *And* David and Duncan took on a new farmhand, who just happened to have been a strapping boy. Vanessa's young son Quentin described David as being very attractive, tall and athletic looking, a physique David made a point of keeping into his sixties, "a sculptural splendour", wrote Quentin.

While Duncan and David were working on the farm they and Vanessa took a lease on a farmhouse, Charleston, located in the village of Firle, Sussex. For the next 50 years Charleston would be the center of Bloomsbury activity, a peaceful haven for not only David, Duncan and Vanessa, but also Julian and Quentin, and would welcome Clive Bell, Keynes, the Stracheys and Roger Fry who designed the gardens, while Duncan carefully selected and nurtured every plant that would be seeded there. The walls, doors and furniture were decorated by Duncan, Vanessa and passing artists, mostly in post-impressionistic style so dear to the heart of Fry, as well as objects from Fry's Omega Workshops. Ponds and statuary were added, as was electricity, but only at the start of the Second World War. Paintings by Duncan and Vanessa adorned the walls, followed later by collections of the works of Stephen Tomlin, Picasso, Renoir and others. Of the gardens Dora Carrington wrote, ''Never, never have I seen quite such a wonderful place!'' In 1936 Vanessa wrote, ''The house seems full of young people in very high spirits, laughing a great deal at their own jokes.''

Clive Bell, Vanessa's husband, Duncan's brief lover and womanizer.

Serious farm work went on, a necessity if they were going to continue as conscientious objectors, and even beehives were added. Duncan had to put up with David's women, as David couldn't live without sexual promiscuity. David wrote to Alix Strachey [the wife of Lytton's largely homosexual brother James] a letter we have thanks to Sarah Knights: ''Duncan is very much in love with me, & if I don't say I am in love with him it is not because I feel less for him than he does for me. I love him & am absolutely dependent on his love. I have never been so happy in my life as in his society. It is the thing of the first importance--the air I breath....'' [so much for ''dull sodomitical twaddle''].

As the reader certainly knows, in a love affair one person always loves more than the other. Normally it was Duncan that boys drooled over, in which case Duncan took advantage of his dominant position by thinking nothing of taking on other lovers. Now it was Duncan who was suffering, and David felt that Duncan's love for him was so strong and limitless that he could exercise his right as a Bloomsbury Setter to bed whomever he wished, occasionally men, more often women. Things got so bad that Duncan threatened suicide, something for David to take seriously because suicide was nearly a cult during that time, as we saw in the first chapter with the deaths of Dora Carrington, Virginia Woolf, Josette Coatmellec, Mark Gertler and Michael Davies \ Rupert Buxton. But the threats put David in an impossibly stressful situation, and in the end served no purpose, as David continued to jump from bed to bed, and Duncan only demeaned himself.

During this period Duncan, despite his complaints concerning David's promiscuity, was also sowing the four winds, including Vanessa Bell who had just given birth to Duncan's child, over whose crib David vowed to later marry ''it''. The eventual marriage would be one of true love between David and Angelica. That David could make such a vow, concerning a wrinkled, nearly hairless baby, seems to indicate that in David's mind she would be the go-between that would cement forever David and Duncan's love.

David decided to open a bookshop with Frankie, a plan that would get him away from the countryside and back to London, and provide both with a living. As for Duncan, the new baby, the wear-and-tear of David's womanizing, and the prospect of sexual encounters with boys who would appreciate him more than did David, forced a wedge between the two men, and now that Duncan's promise to father Vanessa's baby had been fulfilled, the ever-virile and still youthful Duncan made up for the time he'd felt sorry for himself. He also moved back to London, to a new studio, and his preference for painting boys nude [many of them paid hustlers] went far in offering him occasions to have quasi-limitless sex. During one such session David came upon him in the naked embrace of Edward Wolfe, a sight that rendered David sick with jealousy.

It was perhaps in part to put his mind on other things that David wrote a book about his experiences with the cocaine-hooked prostitute, a book he called *Dope-Darling*, which sold surprisingly well. Maynard Keynes came back into his life, Keynes who played a vital role in the lives of many Bloomsbury members. Keynes was becoming hugely influential in financial circles and had used his power to obtain conscientious-objector status for both David and Duncan. He now took steps to ensure that David and Frankie's new bookshop got off on the right footing by providing them with badly needed advice as neither knew anything about commerce, and indeed were said to have felt guilty each time they made a profit. Also thanks to

Keynes and his diaries we have an intimate look into backroom carnality of the male members of the Bloomsbury Set. He systematically listed the number of his sexual encounters, the number of boys he jerked off, the frequency of his being penetrated, and the size of the instruments down to the half-inch, all thanks to Keynes's craze for numbers.

A final word concerning Frankie. The reader may remember that the wife of Roy Campbell had fallen in love with Vita Sackville-West, Virginia Woolf's lover, which caused him to flee to Toledo Spain with his family. Well, Vita was a novelist who later married author and diplomat Harold Nicolson, whose lover was Raymond Mortimer, Mortimer who was Frankie's love-interest and who cared for Frankie during the last year of his life while dying of a brain tumor at age 46. [There are no instances of *uncomplicated* sex and friendships in the Bloomsbury Set.]

Harold and Vita had an open Bloomsbury-style marriage during which Harold, a diplomat and son of a diplomat, had to admit to her that he'd contracted a venereal disease picked up through an anonymous homosexual encounter. Vita was as sexually free, although Harold felt she went too far when she eloped with a certain Violet Trefusis and Harold was obliged to go to France to fetch her back, writing in his journal, ''Damn! Damn! Damn! Violet. How I *loathe* her.'' He and Vita wrote each other daily when separated by his foreign postings and her wanderlust, and he retired early to be with her more often. A Francophile, he was greatly loved in France when, returning there after the war, he fell to his knees and kissed the earth. ''When a Frenchman asked the prostrate Nicolson *"Monsieur a laissé tomber quelque-chose?"* ("Sir, have you dropped something?"), Nicolson replied *"Non, j'ai retrouvé quelque-chose"* (No, I have recovered something"), a quote taken from Wikipedia. Harold became a writer, as was his wife, publishing the life of Verlaine, among other books. He knew everyone, and his diaries are considered inestimable. He and Vita had two sons, one of whom wrote *A Portrait of a Marriage*, his parents'.

I will end David Garnett's life here, to be partially taken up again in the chapter on Duncan Grant. He had two sons by a first wife, and four daughters by Duncan's child Angelica. He continued on in his bookshop, he wrote books of his own and founded the very successful Nonesuch Press. He continued having affairs with girls and boys, he was always genuine as a person, a genuine charmer. He separated from Angelica and moved to France where he died at age 89.

CHAPTER FOUR

ROGER FRY

Roger Fry, 1866-1934, was introduced into the Bloomsbury Set by Vanessa Bell and was highly appreciated by her sister Virginia Woolf who said of Fry, "He had more knowledge and experience than the rest of us put together." He was deeply in love with Vanessa, was her lover, and immensely hurt when she asked Fry's lover at the time, Duncan Grant, with whom she was in love, to sire her child, the future Angelica, after which Duncan and Vanessa lived together as brother and sister for 40 years. Vanessa's husband Clive Bell called Fry a genius and traveled with him to Paris, both lovers, in search of new talent for the exhibitions Fry was thinking of mounting [they found droves (11)]. Because Vanessa knew of her sister Virginia's love for Fry, she had tried to keep Fry and her affair between themselves, without success: "Virginia told me last night that she suspected me of having a liaison with you. She has been quick to suspect it, hasn't she?" Virginia's biographers suggest that her knowledge of the affair played a major role in her decision to accept Leonard Woolf as a runner-up candidate for husband. About Fry Virginia later wrote: With Roger Fry there was "always some new idea afoot ... always some new picture standing on a chair to be looked at, some new poet to be fished out of obscurity and stood in the light of day."

Fry and Duncan, in the only picture we have of them together [sorry!]. About Duncan Fry wrote, "He pleases because he is so unconstrained, so entirely natural and unaffected. His naturalness gives him his singular charm and manner." In his book on Duncan, published in 1923, Fry forgot to mention that they had been lovers.

Fry had been married and had had a daughter and son before his wife had to be committed to a mental institution. His affairs were largely with women, the most important of whom was Helen Anrep, twenty years younger, who left her husband to care for Fry until the end of his life.

Another woman, Josette Coatmellec, followed Fry through his displacements, complaining that he loved his art more than he cared for her, something that Fry denied in a letter, a letter that arrived too late, as she shot herself.

Fry was the son of a judge, a wealthy Quaker. He studied at Clifton College and King's College, Cambridge, Paris and Rome where he learned painting, the first step to his becoming an art critic. Somerset Maugham once said about his writing talent, ''I know just where I stand: in the very front row of the second-rate.'' Fry was as honest about his own painting ability. He did portraits and landscapes about which he said, I ''am a serious artist with *some* sensibility and taste'' [my emphasis]. He considered Cowdray Park his best painting.

Cowdray Park and Cowdray Cottage by Roger Fry.

He founded *The Burlington Magazine*, the first periodical on art history in Britain, and wrote hundreds of articles covering everything from children's drawings to bushman art. He became Curator of Paintings at the Metropolitan Museum of Art in N.Y. [MOMA] and from 1910 organized exhibitions in London that led to Londoners' discovery of Cezanne, Manet, Matisse, van Gogh, Seurat and Picasso, all of whose art was so undervalued by the public that his reputation as an art critic was seriously damaged [one critic suggesting that he join his wife in her asylum]. The art critic for *The Daily Telegraph* wrote that he ''threw down his catalogue and stamped on it''. All of which is as unfathomable to us today as the fisticuffs that broke out during the first presentation of Stravinsky's *Le Sacre du printemps*. But later exhibitions received fewer insults, as confirmed by David Boyd Haycock in his book *Crisis of Brilliance*, 2009: ''Fry's second exhibition was not as badly received as the first. The intervening two years had seen a number of avant-garde shows in London. The art world was suddenly awash with *isms*.'' Haycock wrote, concerning the Bloomsbury Set: ''It was a thrilling moment, the coming together of a circle of glittering talents who would help to refashion England's literary and artistic culture for the next forty years, dragging it into the world of Modern." [David Boyd Haycock was a writer whose biographies include the lives of Dora Carrington and Mark Gertler, the painter who wanted to commit suicide when Carrington chose to sleep with homosexuals rather than with him.]

Fry founded the Omega Workshops in London in 1913, the aim of which was to interest young artists in the design and decoration of everyday functional objects, fire screens, lampshades, tables and fabric designs. The Workshops provided a working space for those of different horizons and an "income for talented but hungry artists", said Gretchen Gerzina, who also wrote a book on the life of Dora Carrington.

He became attached to Goldsworthy Lowes Dickinson, then a young political science lecturer. Called Goldie, Dickinson was in love with Roger Frey whom he bedded despite Dickinson's philosophy based on Platonic Neo-Platonism. Goldie entered the boarding school of Beomonds, then Charterhouse School, from ages 14 to 19, followed by King's College, Cambridge. In 1896 he wrote *The Greek View of Life*. E.M. Forster wrote the biography of Dickinson after Dickinson's death in 1932 but omitted all information concerning Dickinson's homosexuality and foot fetishism. Dickinson had been involved in both the Apostles and the Bloomsbury Set. He wrote dozens of books, one of which was *The Magic Flute: A Fantasia* to *Plato and his Dialogues*. His relationships with young men like Fry were both sexual and fatherly, certainly an ideal figure for a boy needing warm guidance from a man who would show him the way, instructing him intellectually while satisfying him tenderly and physically, yet without the virile dimension so vital in Ancient Greece.

Dickinson was reputed as having been remarkably candid in exposing Platonic homoerotism by stating, "That there was another side to the matter goes without saying. This passion, like any other, has its depths, as well as its heights"--daring for the times, apparently. Paul Robinson summarized Dickinson's sexual life as "an intensely romantic attachment, passionate kisses and warm embraces [with a hint of fetishism (feet)], followed by relief by masturbation." Dickinson himself confessed to masturbating, when young, over his father's boots.

Forster was handicapped in what he could write because homosexuality was illegal when his book on Dickinson came out in 1934, and any revelations could have seriously damaged the reputations of his friends. [The Buggery Act of 1533 punished homosexual acts with death; the death penalty was removed in 1861; a limited decriminalization was voted in 1967; the age of consent was lowered from age 21 to age 18 in 1994; and in the year 2000 it was lowered to age 16.]

Finally, Dickinson wrote that for those whose ideal was young men, King's College, Cambridge, was ideal.

Goldie Dickinson

Fry was a tutor at the Slade School of Art, Dora Carrington and Mark Gertler among his students. A fellow Slade teacher, Henry Tonks, was not impressed by the articles Fry wrote for his *Burlington Magazine* and said that surely Fry ''might find something more interesting to talk about than Bushmen''. Tonks, who had had a career as a surgeon before switching to painting, told his students that he couldn't stop them from going to Fry's exhibitions but added that they could avoid the risk on contamination by staying away [he would later change his mind and his paintings became highly impressionistic, exposed today in the Tate Gallery].

Roger Fry was an enthralling lecturer, ''with a deep, mellifluous voice''', wrote his biographer Anne-Pascale Bruneau, and could fill the 2000-seat auditorium of Queen's Hall. Frances Marshal Partridge [whom we meet later in the chapter on Lytton Strachey] wrote that ''anyone who heard Roger Fry lecture on art must owe him an immense debt of pure pleasure, for he had the rare gift of conveying his own love of painting.'' Fry's books include the lives of Giovanni Bellini, Cézanne and Henri Matisse.

He suffered a fall in 1934, which led to a heart attack two days later. Virginia Woolf wrote, ''I feel dazed; very wooden. My head is stiff. I think the poverty of life now is what comes to me; and this blackish veil over everything.''

A Fry self-portrait and an example of his art. Historian Frances Spalding wrote, "It was Roger who fully unleashed Vanessa's sexual passion."

CHAPTER FIVE

GEORGE MALLORY

Boarding School Sexuality

George Mallory, 1886-1924, was the son of a well-off clergyman and his younger brother was a W.W. II Air Force Commander named Trafford. At age 13 Mallory won a scholarship in mathematics to Winchester College where one of his teachers, R.L.G. Irving took him and a select group mountain climbing in the Alps each year. He went to Cambridge in 1905 and became intimate with the Bloomsbury Set, including the Strachey brothers--homosexual James and Lytton, Rupert Brooke, Maynard Keynes and Duncan Grant. Of Mallory Lytton Strachey wrote, "*Mon dieu*--George Mallory! He's six foot high, with the body of an athlete by Praxiteles, and a face--Oh incredible--the mystery of Botticelli, the refinement and the delicacy of a Chinese print, the youth and piquancy of an unimaginable English boy." All of these men were homosexual, as was Mallory. Duncan was his lover for a short period and James Strachey gave in only after Mallory forced himself on him [literally *begging* him]. Lytton Strachey failed to gain access to Mallory, although he tried, and tried and tried again. Rupert Brooke's love life remains too enigmatic to known if he'd slept with the mountaineer.

Mallory by Duncan Grant.

At age 9 Mallory entered the Winchester preparatory boarding school, one that had such an effect on his sexuality that we will take a second diversion into a British institution which altered the lives of every student who, in one way or another, has ruled England since Henry VIII.

Oxford and Cambridge are referred to together as Oxbridge, schools for the rich and aristocratic where the dons, following a Middle-Ages custom, were not married, but where an inexhaustible supply of highborn boys were at their disposal. Lads were trained academically and homosexually on courses of Greek and Latin classics, the first step of which were the prep schools of Repton, Harrow, Winchester and others. Of disputed educational value in the past, today Oxbridge rank in the top 5 of the world's universities, and many of the schools that prepare students for entrance into Oxbridge are often, intellectually, *today*, the *crème de la crème*.

Oxbridge were ruled by dons, professors who lived in the upper-class world they created in their image, exclusive, privileged to an unbelievable extend because they could do as they pleased with university monies, live in lavish surroundings, kowtowed to like emperors by teachers and staff.

Margaret Thatcher ended their paradise in the 1980s by asking the question What-the-hell-are-they-doing with Britain's money?, and, when she found out, she put a stop to it.

Cambridge was founded in 1209 by scholars fleeing Oxford because of disputes between the great Henry II's far-less-great son King John and Pope Innocent III, as to who should appoint the Archbishop of Canterbury. In 1231 both Oxford and Cambridge received charters from Henry III which freed them from paying taxes, as well as the right, accorded by Pope Gregory IX, for graduates to teach wherever they wished.

During the Middle Ages grammar, rhetoric, logic, mathematics, geometry and astrology were taught, augmented with mind-liberating Humanities during the Renaissance. Six new colleges were added to Cambridge between 1430 and 1496, for a total of 31 today. With the

Reformation Henry VIII named Cambridge don Thomas Cranmar as the first Protestant Archbishop of Canterbury, who was soon afterwards beheaded by the Catholic Queen Mary. The Cambridge teacher William Tyndale translated the Bible into English, and because the Bible was exclusively the church's domain, he was burned at the stake.

Cambridge men were among the Pilgrims that founded America and Cambridge graduate John Harvard endowed the university that adopted his name. Cambridge Oliver Cromwell saw to the beheading of Charles I.

Isaac Newton was a Fellow of Trinity College who didn't believe in the religious Trinity but was personally supported by Charles II who left him free to discover his laws of motion and gravity, in addition to calculus, and tell men that although God set all in motion, He had other things to do than the day-to-day running of the universe, thereby freeing men's minds to look into the subject themselves.

Cambridge man Francis Bacon was making progress in science while giving his lover Buckingham advice as to how to manipulate *his* lover James I/VI. The Cambridge atheist Halley was discovering his comet, while people began to talk about the Cambridge student Charles Darwin--and have never stopped.

The Enlightenment at an end, women were allowed into Oxford in 1869 and into Cambridge in 1920, although without full rights until 1947. The likes of the Bloomsbury Set set the pace afterwards.

The Society of Apostles was formed at Cambridge in 1820 where homosexually physical friendships were formed, called Lower Sodomy, or what was called Higher Sodomy, non-sexual male bonding. Society members created, later, the Bloomsbury Set. As mentioned, Mallory was associated with the Apostles, and took advantage of both its scholastic and homoerotic elements.

Schools were homosexual settings in the 1800s where the highborn went to do boys, where learning was far less important than playing both musical beds and sports, the athletic heroes of which were chosen to be Fag Masters and had their pick of the prettiest lads, employing them to bring them off manually or lying on their stomachs, and whose influence was reinforced by handing the lads, post-orgasm, to their friends for their personal gratification. Among themselves, in their own dormitories, the young boys continued their inexhaustible sexual hijinks which John Symonds called ruthless orgies. Symonds wailed against the abuse of boys by headmasters, yet purportedly had sex with a choirboy, William Fear Dyer, and in addition was forced to flee to Switzerland when accused by his private student Shorting of aiding Shorting in Shorting's pursuit of the choirboy Walter Thomas Goolden. Symonds always claimed to have practiced High Sodomy, for example having loved his pupil Norman Moor but without having sex with him, although Symonds wrote in his diary, ''I stripped him naked and fed sight, touch and mouth on these things,'' which means what it means, and is the reason why when boys became men they formed pacts with their friends to burn their papers, diaries and other proofs of pederasty that could tarnish their earthly reputations. Symonds was an example of repressed, sexually unsatisfied poofs, in stark contrast to those like Byron who exulted in their physical possession of an unlimited number of young asses, Bryon claiming to have had full intercourse with 200 in Greece during just one trip, coming down and nearly dying of fever, probably *not* the result of homosexual exhaustion, although Byron did write that he was so sated he envisioned an extended halt to any form of lovemaking (4).

Getting back to the sexually unsatisfied Symonds: like so many Brits who drooled over Italian boys--similar to Ashenbach in Thomas Mann's *Death in Venice*--Symonds too breathed his last in the city of the Doges [his papers later burned by Edmund Gosse], although Symonds did write this, that has come down to us, concerning Jonathan and David:

> In his arms of strength
> And in that kiss
> Soul into soul was knit
> And bliss to bliss.

In tandem with the mediocrity of an education in both Oxford and Cambridge, was the poor physical condition of the writers, poets and other aesthetes, of the 1800s and early 1900s, that frequented both schools. Yet they were convinced of their excellence, even if many were nothing but arrogant wimps, often moneyed, who paid for rent-boys in pre-W.W. II Germany and Italy, an easy task in those years where a lad would sell himself for the proverbial Hersey Bar [after the war most boys sold themselves for even less because they were *starving*] (4). Many Oxbridge boys didn't see war because they were physically unfit to be induced, poor eyesight, bird-breasted chests, precocious varicose-veins, girlish biceps. The exceptions were spectacular: Rupert Brooke, Byron and several others, yet even Byron was only attractive when illness brought his weight down to human levels. Few of the men from Oxford and Cambridge resembled the boys seen in gymnasiums or on the wrestling mats, although the boys they paid for were often physically splendid. Proud of the clothes they donned for extravagant meals and the robes they wore in the inner chambers of their rooms, coquettish and swishy, they wouldn't have turned on even a girl, let alone far more demanding males--effeminate twits that make England, today, the last place virile males seek out their own, although there are, and have always been, remarkable exceptions. The writer Wyndham Lewis called Duncan Grant ''a little fairy-like individual who would have received no attention in any country except England." In a nutshell, that's exactly what I'm talking about. Which is why the English themselves look to other lands for good sex.

Tutors and students took sherry together and shared meals, after which what naturally happened when young men wished to please their masters did happen, consisting most probably of little more than mutual masturbation, but when it took place one time it was hard to see how the inexperienced student could [or would dare to] ward off a second and then a third occasion, and so on, which meant, in the end, that it was a disgraceful debasement of what should have been a striving towards academic excellence. It was putrid exploitation, exploitation that Mallory may have had to agree to under his tutor Arthur Benson, as will be seen. In the Greek way the lover served as a tutor, whose quest was to instruct the boy as well as sexually share acts of love, but the difference was that the boy always chose the man, and that the man was but a few years older, handsome thanks to boys being physically trained, from childhood, to care for their bodies, whereas in Cambridge and Oxford the tutors were flabby, pale-skinned, often androgynous wrecks. We know nothing of Byron's sexual encounters with his tutors, although they most certainly took place, but we do known he had the consolation of lads younger than he, for whom his experience, eloquence, fine clothes, wealth, title and tastes made him a god, a god who willingly released them from their virginity if they had managed to keep it till then, which, knowing boarding schools that catered to lads 12 and over, was highly improbable.

About his own schooling, John Addington Symonds wrote: "The talk in the dormitories and studies was of the grossest character, with repulsive scenes of onanism, mutual masturbation and obscene orgies of naked boys in bed together. There was no refinement, just animal lust." The first order that Makepeace Thackeray received on his first day at school from a schoolmate was "Come & frig me," he wrote later.

How much the men who left both universities, to become truly great warriors and administrators, owed to Oxford and Cambridge training cannot of course be known, but there were many who thought that bonding through the exchange of sexual favors was destined to ready the graduates for their role as builders and leaders of the British Empire, an inane belief but one supported, in a way, by Plato who had Aristophanes put this in one of his plays: "While they are boys they love men and like to lie with them and embrace them, and these are the best of the boys and youths. The evidence is that it's these boys, when they grow up, who become the best men in politics."

Many of these aristocratic pansies were in no way comparable to the admirable *men* who died at Thermopylae and in the ranks of the Sacred Band of Thebes, nor those who fought in the Crimea and Gallipoli, who ruled the seas for generations and made the second most populous country in the world, India, a democracy, who were decimated in the First World War and saved England from disaster in the Second, and most assuredly had nothing to do with the homosexual trio of fops, Blunt, Burgess and Maclean, who betrayed their country to the murderous Soviets.

The first English school was thought to have been establish in 598 A.D., the purpose of which was to produce those who ran the church, and as the members were priests they were also celibate, a tradition that continued later on, encompassing the first university dons. The nobility was educated in Latin in which the Bible was written, although the curriculum was extended to rhetoric, mathematics, astronomy and music, exactly the same classes taught in ancient Rome, which were carbon copies of those in earlier Greece. As pure, unbroken voices were necessary for church services, boys from every horizon were recruited, especially among the poor, boys who were offered the rudiments of an education, free of charge, boys who filled the countless ranks of those sexually used by the celibates who ran the schools. Convinced in one way or another that they were accomplishing part of God's will, little convincing was necessary to have them bend over. Later thousands of men became priests thanks to the infinite pool of boys that made up the church, from the very first schools right up to today's, religious institutions where, for some recondite reason, the church can keep clericals out of prison simply by paying damages. For the boys, historically, this was nonetheless their ticket out of poverty, many becoming church clericals and boy abusers in their own time.

While nobles were taught at home by private tutors, the poor were welcomed into schools like Eton that Henry VIII set up in 1442 to provide pre-pubescent lads for his choirs. Dozens of schools were founded by Henry and Elizabeth on the ashes of those destroyed in order for the Anglican church to reign supreme.

Because schools were far between, boys eventually became boarders in towns around the schools. This was easily accepted because the nobles had farmed out their boys to be educated in the houses of other nobles for years, at around age 7. Eventually it was realized that these fee-paying lads could become a huge source of profit if they were housed in schools. This helped too for disciplinary reasons as the closer the boys were physically to their tutors, the easier it was to control them. Thus the advent of boarding schools. Soon an incredible *esprit de corps* formed between the boys, meaning that a boy interviewed for a job by someone who had been to his college was nearly certain to be hired. And it was not uncommon that boys dying in war had a last thought for their college house before that of their God. When the tenderness of first love is mingled with all the other first experiences of life, an inherent part of youth, no armed concrete is more solid.

The early schools were based on Latin and scriptures, Greek and the classics came later, during the Renaissance. And although England was making incredible strides in exploration, discovery, rule over other lands, advances in medicine under Harvey and science under Newton, public schools continued on as arrogant social functions aimed at showing off one's eccentricities in fine clothing, to honor the best in food and wines, and to have free, unsuppressed and unlimited sexual access to new boys entering each year. Nothing the world has known could compete with the wild orgiastic no-holds-barred sex in the entirely unsupervised dormitories. Moreover, boys slept two to a bed in the first boarding schools, until 1805 at Harrow. No wonder men would later die with the burning memory of youthful lust alive in their breasts like incandescent coals, and why men, become fathers, tolerated nearly every excess in their sons, an exclusively British phenomenon, and the reason that once a Brit ended his school years he exiled himself for extended and numerous visits to more liberal skies, especially those of Italy and pre-W.W. II Germany, while in Britain homosexuality was punished by death until 1835, when the last man was beheaded.

As there were few masters in the early schools to control hundreds of lads, beatings were among the most appalling to have existed, and they and other forms of abuse have continued right up to the present as the reader will soon see. Floggings by headmasters inspired cruelty among the boys, and even Bertrand Russell wrote that the big boys hit him so he hit the little boys, "that's fair", he concluded.

Dormitories were no more than male brothels. To make sex easy and accessible, [a healthy boy being able to ejaculate six times daily], the linings of their pockets were cut away so they could play with themselves, even in class, but two boys could especially practice mutual masturbation, withdrawing their hands from the other's pocket in a second if interrupted. For unknown reasons homosexuality was more fashionable in some schools than others, and even in schools where it was fashionable it suddenly ceased being so, whereas where it was little practiced it might come back with a bang. In one school a headmaster who succeeded in rounding up a huge number of boys, said to have been around 100, and having them all beaten for some forgotten rascality, was applauded by the boys afterwards for having been clever enough to catch them all.

It would seem that the earlier boys start having sex among themselves, the easier sex is throughout their lives. On the other hand, boys who enter into sexual relations with girls later on are more stressful and fearful, and the sexual satisfaction is far less to what they had known with other boys at puberty. The result is unhappy marriages and divorce. Sex is easy between boys because they are simply clones of each other; there is little that is unfamiliar for them to discover; they've known from puberty what turns them on.

The holidays in those early schools were short, 20 to 30 days a year from 1500 to 1700, while the academic part of the day was short, 4 hours at Eton in the 1750s, half-days on Thursdays and on Saturdays, and no schooling at all Tuesdays and Sundays.

But the age was brutal--the 1600s and 1700s--when sailors were lashed to death, parents were cruel to their children, children could be imprisoned for stealing a handkerchief, poor houses where children were beaten and exposed to every form of sexual vice, several children to a bed, and where headmasters were told explicitly by parents to birch them at their first obstinacy. It was a time when children were farmed out to wet nurses until around age 7 when, if they hadn't died of a childhood disease as at least half did, they were packed off to boarding schools. An example: like Byron, Talleyrand had had a clubfoot and had been sent to poor provincials to be brought up without the slightest education. Miraculously, a relative discovered him and took him to Paris to the rich residence of his parents where he and the boy walked in on a party of wigged noblemen, Talleyrand in filthy rags, bringing an immediate end to the chamber music and festivities. ''This is your son!'' the relative bellowed to the amazed parents.

Abuse in schools could go on unhampered because the headmasters washed their hands at what went on between the lads, especially as they knew they couldn't control it, and because they had their own lives to lead. The fact that boys were in class for so few hours gave them acres of free time, and nowhere was the saying idle hands are the devil's workshop more true. Their parents bought their own freedom by dispatching the boys to schools, giving them enough money to buy the drink and food and whores they coveted, rampaging through the streets, free to wreak havoc because the towns people could not complain to headmasters who would do nothing, nor the boys' parents who were most often their betters and who resided far away. *And* the money jingling in the lads' pockets would eventually find its way into town shops.

Education in these schools was wholly secondary to the comfort and prestige of the place parents parked their children, and such academic dinosaurs would have disappeared eons ago had it not been for the fact that they evolved, and thanks to their wealth are now able to hire the best teachers who give the best education, and today rank among the world's top institutions. In public schools the sanction is immediate: when a school drops in rank its rich subscribers turn elsewhere, while *state* schools go on and on, no matter how mediocre the instruction. Luckily for America its universities are so wealthy the students are admitted through exams, meaning that the poorest church mouse can become a veritable pillar of society, even if the vast majority of the students are prepared by the best

American prep schools, something out of the reach of all but the most dedicated, hard-working poor. Yet the tradition of starting off cleaning school toilets and ending up the school dean [in America, of course] still [I hope] prevails.

The attitude today, sexually, is that boys can do what they want as long as they are discreet and there is no sexual exploitation, a form of don't ask/don't tell. And that's the way it should be. Boys should be left alone, in the sense that adults must be excluded because they can force boys by their positions [priests and headmasters], their sweet talk [as men are infinitely more experienced and knowledgeable than boys], money and other forms of pressure and coercion. The rule of older boys poses a conundrum because young lads can be drawn to their prowess, especially when they're successful athletes. Older boys can show responsibility in the Greek way, become a teacher and protector, encouraging the boy to greater heights. In that case, who can rightfully cast the first stone?

About Winchester Mallory wrote to his parents: ''It's simply lovely here; life is like a dream.'' At Winchester he became an athlete, excelling in group sports like soccer and cricket, and was the school's best gymnast, thanks to which he developed the Praxiteles body so admired by Lytton Strachey. Another boy described him as ''smooth-chinned, pre-Raphaelite-looking young man''. At Winchester he was introduced to a school master who took him climbing in the Alps during the summer, Andrew Irving, 27, Mallory 17. Of Mallory Irving later wrote: ''He had a strikingly beautiful face. Its shape, its delicately cut features, especially the heavily lashed thoughtful eyes, were extraordinarily suggestive of a Botticelli Madonna.'' They spent weeks in the mountains together, just the two of them. This, Irving repeated with other boys, over a period of five years. Then, in 1930, two of his young climbers fell to their deaths, and his days of mountain climbing with boys came to an end.

Andrew Irving

Mallory went to Oxford in 1905, majoring in History. His tutor was Arthur Benson, there to guide his studies during three of his four years at the college. Benson found Mallory ''a fine looking boy'' and was struck by the ''extraordinary and delicate beauty of his face,'' quotes brought to us by Peter and Leni Gillman in their excellent *The Wildest Dream*, 2000. ''A singular, more ingenuous, more unaffected, more genuinely interesting boy I never saw. He is to be under me, and I rejoice in the thought,'' commented Benson. It was apparently Benson who introduced the boy to the Bloomsbury Set, and all it encompassed.

Mallory by Duncan Grant

Benson was homosexual, a man who strongly believed ''in friendships 'across the generations' which brought together 'youth and age' '', the Gillmans tell us. ''He went further, referring to 'romantic attachments' which were to be conducted with 'seemliness and decorum'.'' Men who have power over the young, whom the young need to advance, scholastically, was the disgusting legacy of those times in Oxford, Cambridge and elsewhere. How hard Benson pushed himself on Mallory, and how far Mallory allowed him to go, can of course never by known.

A photo of Mallory taken by Duncan Grant. Mallory asked Grant for copies of the photos he took, stating, ''I am profoundly interested in the nude me.''

Benson introduced Mallory to Charles Sayle, a homosexual and intimate friend of Rupert Brooke and Maynard Keynes, who in turn introduced Mallory to the Apostles. Charles Sayle later claimed that Mallory had become one of his swans, code for his having given himself to Sayle. Sayle was the founder of the Climbers' Club in which Mallory organized a trip to the mountains in North Wales, in the company of three of Sayler's other swans, one of whom was Rupert Brooke, the others George Keynes and Hugh Wilson. A high point of the climb was when they all bathed naked together after a day's efforts, as photographs he took testify. George Keynes wrote that ''They were the best days of my life.'' Mallory's younger brother Trafford had begged to come along, but Mallory refused--one wonders why? Mallory then joined a rowing club with Rupert Brooke.

Mallory was homosexually active, and thanks to the above material I've presented one can easily see that he didn't lack in easily accessible bodies, as everyone was not only doing it, ''it'' was ''in'', and to not participate left one out of liberal university and academic society. One could claim that he participated because he was obliged to do so, wishing not to be a social pariah. The truth seems that Mallory was an enthusiastic, perhaps a leading, character in what went on in the Bloomsbury Set, and we know that his sexual presence was sought by Duncan Grant, the Strachey brothers, the Keynes brothers, and numerous boys on the skirts of the Set. The pleasure was amplified because there was always an element of conquest, of the gradually-building-up arousal that followed from one's first meeting, to the final conclusion in the warmth of a shared bed. The conquest of a boy was not unlike the conquest of Everest, the exciting part being the preparation and the scaling. There were no saunas and bathhouses used for sexual encounters back then, no possibility of instantly meeting and mating as today, on the streets, in gyms, swimming pools and porno cinemas; and picking up someone in a park could get a man hanged until 1885, imprisoned afterwards. The ease of sex today can also be compared to Everest today, where those with money can literally get themselves all but carried to the summit of the peak.

Mallory posed in the nude, and not only for Grant Duncan, and one can be certain that what went on before and afterwards involved a shared orgasm. The true mystery is why biographers should try to hide or explain away ["adolescent curiosity", "a passing bisexuality"] what has been perfectly natural since before, far before, the Ancient Greeks. Mallory was part and parcel of the intellectually advanced among us, a man who accepted himself and life for what it was. That he married may have been a normal outcome of the omnisexuality that has existed up to our own complicated heterosexual-or-homosexual age. On the other hand, he may have been pushed by Victorian societal pressures to do so, which was very often the case in that time, especially if one had a reputation to maintain, and marriage was proof of normality. Then again, he may have been genuinely omnisexual. The Greeks preferred boys but copulated easily with women (5), and the Spartans were even obliged to do so in order to produce the soldiers who would one day stand for them as they now stood for their officers (6). The Romans were completely omnisexual, taking what happened to be at hand, be it a male or female slave (7). Afterwards, religion put the mark of Satan on anything to do with homosexuality, even when priests often became priests due to the easy access to choirboys. Mallory's form of omnisexuality is the path of the future, when boys can decide with whom they'll share their bed for the night, thanks to that infallible compass, the direction that points their erect phallus--meaning it hardens in the presence of what truly sexually stimulates him, be it a boy or a girl or both.

James Strachey was extremely candid about his relations with Mallory. He wrote that Mallory "insisted, before we parted, on copulating. He seemed so very anxious, I submitted." The experience hadn't been a good one for James, and later Mallory tried to remain his friend by writing him, "You had better forget that I was ever your lover."

James Strachey by Duncan Grant.

He met Geoffrey Winthrop Young, a mountaineer and Eton and Cambridge graduate, a man who preferred rough-trade, especially boxers, and Mallory. In 1909 they went off to the Alps together, for a few months of climbing, including a stay at Chamonix.

Geoffrey Winthrop Young

When Mallory graduated from Oxford his dream was to become a teacher at Winchester, but the headmaster appears to have told him that he was not teacher material. He was offered a position at the prep school Charterhouse, teaching History, Math, Latin and French. James's older brother Lytton Strachey tried to bed Mallory at Charterhouse itself, but James wrote that Mallory got out of it by saying there would be no place private enough at Charterhouse. Everyone who knew Mallory knew that when he wanted someone he *always* found both the time and place. Lytton himself wrote Duncan Grant: ''The copulation never come. I would have given worlds for an embrace.'' In another letter to Grant, Lytton wrote: ''I reached here yesterday in a state bordering on collapse,'' due to his inability to seduce Mallory.

Mallory went on his sixth trip to the Alps in 1912, during which there were three deaths, the bodies found by his lover Geoffrey Young, about one of which Young wrote, "He looked like a young god, lying at rest on a rock after bathing." With the equipment they had, mountaineering was insanely dangerous, and took place only because of the recklessness of youth. Boys wore tweeds [some wore ties!] and thick boots, ropes were made of easily ruptured hemp and attached to any outcropping, while pitons weren't even invented until 1920 [and were then shunned as being unmanly, an artificial means of cheating]. One had simply to slip, or to lose a grip on a rock, in order to fall to one's death. The use of duck down was just being experimented with.

In 1912 Maynard Keynes was now well-off enough to book an entire hotel, the Crown in Everleigh, where Duncan, Rupert Brooke, Dilly Knox [introduced later] and others, a score of men and women, had an orgy during which Keynes, who loved Rupert, had to witness him screwing a *girl*.

As Irving had done when Mallory was a student, Mallory now too began to take students on climbs, all of whom were the personification of beauty, magnificent specimens of British manhood.

Mallory, on the left, and Siegfried Herford, an example of British beauty, 1914.

Boots worn at the time, these found on Mallory's dead body.

Sex between boys is easy because boys are carbon copies of each other. They know exactly what to do sexually. This rarely goes beyond sexual discovery and experimentation in countries that do not have boarding schools because societal pressures literally push boys into the arms of girls. But in British dormitories what followed sexual discovery was years of sexual intimacy, with only minor exploration with girls that a lad could pay for, and only those with a serious heterosexual bent chose to pay for what they could get for free each night thanks to their roommates. What was easy among themselves became far more complicated on that unknown continent which was women. Everything, there, had to be learned anew, and psychologists maintain that boys who have not known girls from the very start of their sexuality will never experience the fullness of love, the intensity of orgasm, that they knew nightly with boys. Public college boys who married were rarely fully sexually content, and either they had boys on the side or they depended heavily on masturbatory skills.

Mallory met Ruth Turner and they married in 1915. The love was most certainly sincere on both sides, even if, the night before the wedding, Mallory bathed nude with Duncan Grant and Geoffrey Young, Young who was also his best man. I'm glad that I've already introduced the notion of *panier de crabes*, because Victorian times were decidedly strange (4), although Ruth most assuredly was a pure soul throughout their marriage.

The war came, and the death of Rupert Brooke. Mallory came through the massacres during his military service, 1916-1918, after which he returned to teaching at Charterhouse.

Everest was designated the highest mountain in the world in 1856, and was named after the surveyor, George Everest. The first man interested in climbing Everest was Francis Younghusband in 1893. In 1921 the Royal Geographic Society decided the time ripe to conquer the mountain, and Mallory was invited, in part thanks to the intervention of Geoffrey Young. Younghusband chaired the Mount Everest Committee, responsible for the planning. The exclusive coverage of the event, sponsored by *The Times,* and royalities on books and photos, brought hope of wealth to the planners. Travel was an immense hassle back then, but far worse were the hazards as yet unknown to the first climbers. The incredibly convoluted glaciers, the terrible heat "radiating from the glacier like a furnace," write the Gillmans, and sun reflected from the ice, all in contrast to freezing temperatures at night. The ridges, the cols, precipices seen and unseen, training the porters--already some Sherpa were treasured like brothers among the climbers; human relations between the men themselves, each an individual often out to advance his own career; quarrels, disputes, but the beauty was such that Mallory wrote, "I have been half the time in ecstasy."

The first attempt fell far short of the goal due to sheer fatigue, the "wind like a hurricane".

Everest in 1922 was put into immediate planning, beginning with a request for Mallory to give a series of lectures on the first attempt, keeping for himself 25% of the proceeds. This time the climbers had better equipment, woolen coats, windbreakers and ski-boots. Compressed oxygen made its appearance because at 29,000 feet there was 1/3rd of the oxygen found at ground level. Mallory viewed oxygen as artificial and a way of cheating. He would change his mind, but not during this trip. [Others argued that "goggles, thermos flasks and warm boots" were just as artificial, note the Gillmans.]

This time the problem was frostbite, from which every man suffered. The leader, George Finch, was also downed by dysentery. Two of the men had tried to use oxygen, thanks to which they had traveled higher than all the others, and during one bitter night in their tents the men discovered they could revive themselves using it.

One last attempt was decided on, this one led by Mallory, two Brits and fourteen porters. It had snowed heavily but their concentration was on reaching the summit, not the avalanche that broke loose from the mountain and buried them all, Mallory having the time to think "the matter was settled." It wasn't for him but seven men were killed. Back in London Mallory was blamed for taking 17 men up the mountain, which "was fifteen too many", wrote a critic. Geoffrey Young offered his compassion, and Younghusband told him he would have led the group in the same way.

Following his return Mallory went back to the lecture circuit, talking to packed houses and receiving 35% of the proceeds, which amply covered what he lost when he left Charterhouse. Still more income came through articles he penned. The circuit went on to N.Y., where pictures of Mallory show him as handsome as ever. He toured eastern America and Canada, then returned to lecture at Cambridge and to prepare the climbing season, 1924.

Despite the avalanche deaths and the opinion of several climbers that Mallory was unqualified to climb Everest, some noting his chronic absentmindedness, his notoriety closed the door on any attempt to exclude him, especially as the expedition had to be a financial success--all of their salaries depended on it--and only Mallory could assure that there would be maximum media coverage.

Ruth and Mallory took a far bigger home, but he could hardly cover the cost of it and that of his growing family. The Everest expedition was in a financial hole too, until a film executive, John Noel, offered £8,000 [£350,000 today] for photographs and film rights.

The major event at the time was the selection of a new team member, and the choice went to a second-year Oxford student, a member of the rowing team, a superb athlete, supremely beautiful, the boy who would perhaps be Mallory's last love, Sandy Irvine, about whom Mallory said he had ''a magnificent body for the job,'' we learn from Julie Summers's book *Fearless on Everest*, 2009.

Mallory and Sandy Irving

Ruth and Mallory's marriage was in an increasingly unhappy state, the finances still bad and Mallory was often away on the lecture circuit, or alone writing, or absent teaching, yet the root cause was that a man could not satisfy himself with a woman or women after having known adolescent first-love in the arms of another boy, the memory and happiness of which would never leave him for long. Mallory's letters to Ruth were extremely loving, but in reality he had little left to offer her, other than facile words and ersatz tenderness. Few men had a sexual side as blatant as Mallory, as testified in his posing for artists and friends nude, and the moment it became warm on an expedition he would strip totally naked, naked among the other fully-dressed trekkers. On trips with friends it was always he who initiated the skinny-dipping, one fully frontal view of him showing a splendid all-boy physique [the image, alas, too poor in quality for publication]. Dressed or naked, with Ruth or no-holds-barred sex with boys, Mallory was not overawed by Victorian modesty. And the letters and diaries left by former lovers prove his lust for the same-sex.

A not so elegant Mallory at right.

Peter and Leni Gillman state that Sandy was ''spectacularly heterosexual'', and, of course, that may have been the case. Biographers seem to sigh with relief when they can prove that the subject of their books put his dick in the right emplacement, a way of according him a clean bill of health. Sandy does come out, concerning Mallory, as a fine young heterosexual man, and as nothing has filtered through concerning his prep-school dormitory years nor his friendships among the famous Oxford Blue Boat rowers, we will accord him the benefit of the doubt, and be pleased that Mallory had the beauty of Everest and the beauty of Sandy before his eyes at the end.

So Mallory's choice of Sandy may have been a one-sided wish to be with the handsomest and by-far youngest member of the climbing team. As the reader knows, nothing in human relationships is more mysterious than men's sexuality, meaning we'll never know if they shared intimate moments together. We do know that on the 6th of June 1924 Mallory and Sandy set off to reach the summit of Mount Everest.

Mallory was found 75 years later. Sandy never.

CHAPTER SIX

E.M. FORSTER

EDWARD CARPENTER

E.M. Forster, 1879-1970, was above all a humanist, acknowledged as such when named President of Cambridge Humanists in 1959 and a member of the British Humanist Association from 1963 until his death in 1970 at age 81. A great aunt left him £800,000 in today's money, which freed him from any form of servitude. He was an on-the-fringe member of Bloomsbury, and a King's College, Cambridge, student. Considered a founding member of the Bloomsbury Set, his name is associated with several men, among them Christopher Isherwood, Benjamin Britten and Roger Fry who said of Carpenter: "Quite one of the best men I have ever met."

His travels took him throughout Europe, especially Italy, which inspired two books, *Where Angels Fear to Tread* and *A Room with a View*. He was secretary to a maharaja and several visits to India inspired his most read book, *A Passage to India*.

Among what is called his "loving relationships" was a very long one with a married policeman.

Forster was nominated for the Nobel Prize 13 times and he wrote his last book at age 35.

Forster

The problem with E.M. Forster's book *Maurice* was that it had a happy ending. Maurice meets a gamekeeper, they fall in love, decide to remain with each other throughout life, *and do so*. Had the book ended in the usual homosexual tragedy Forster might have decided to have it published, as then everyone could plainly see the consequences of immoral love.

The book begins with prep-school boarding-school love and goes on to university love [Greek texts encouraged by horny tutors], the whole apparently based on the true lives of Edward Carpenter, 1844-1929, and his lover George Merrill. It was finally published in 1971, a year after his death, 60 years after its creation.

Interestingly, Maurice tries to cure himself of his love of boys through hypnotism before deciding to be of service to the working class by running a boxing gym, the compensation being the naked lads under the showers.

A humanist like Forster, Edward Carpenter chose to aid the lower classes, as well as finding his sexual companions among them: "the grimy and oil-besmeared figure of a stoker" or "the thick-thighed hot course-fleshed young bricklayer with a strap around his waist." He also doted on Parisian rent-boys.

He decried the industrial smog of Sheffield that was killing thousands and realized that only a strong socialist movement had the potential of putting things right.

Educated at Brighton College and Trinity Hall, Cambridge, at his father's death Carpenter inherited enough to become financially independent. He bought a farm that he worked, while writing his book of poems, *Towards Democracy*.

Carpenter by Roger Fry

He met George Merrill, a working-class man without a formal education, in 1891 at age 47, and they lived together 27 years despite the hysteria due to the Oscar Wilde trial and the Criminal Law Bill that outlawed all forms of homosexual contact. Concerning Merrill he wrote, in his *Intermediate Sex*: "Eros is a great leveller. Perhaps the true Democracy rests, more firmly than anywhere else, on a sentiment which easily passes the bounds of class and caste, and unites in the closest affection the most estranged ranks of society. It is noticeable how often [homosexuals] of good position and breeding are drawn to rougher types, as of manual workers, and frequently very permanent alliances grow up in this way, which although not publicly acknowledged have a decided influence on social institutions, customs and political tendencies." The book was the foundation of the LGBT movement [lesbian, gay, bisexual and transgender].

Merrill and Carpenter.

Carpenter's last years were devoted to homosexual rights, as well as the protection of the environment and animals, the benefits of a vegetarian diet and the necessity of pacifism. George Orwell attacked him as representing ''every fruit-juice drinker, nudist, sandal wearer and sex maniac'' in the Socialist movement.

Merrill died in 1928, bringing on a stroke that kept Carpenter paralyzed until his own death in 1929.

Merrill and Carpenter's tombs.

Forster became a close friend of both men, as did John Addington Symonds and Stephen Spender.

Forster's tombstone.

Edward Carpenter did what he could when writing *The Intermediate Sex*, given the homophobia of the times, the existing laws, and fears that his friends would be open to calumny. The book is very thin and so the copy sent to me, a reprint, is in such huge type [to give it the appearance of being book length] that it's difficult to read! Here are the salient parts:

Carpenter begins by saying that all women have a dash of men in them and vice-versa, which means that today both sexes are drawing nearer, both appreciating music, art and bicycling.

The intermediate sex is a man like any other, healthy, well-developed, muscular, with a powerful brain and a high standard of conduct [Carpenter is describing, of course, his conception of himself]. They do not necessarily force themselves to marry and have children, and if they do marry it is often platonically [as several Bloomsbury men did].

Those who realize what they are homosexual have serious inner struggles, particularly because they share the emotional soul-nature of women, even though, he stresses again, they are every bit as masculine as other men in body and mind.

Men who take to them are lucky "as they walk on roses without ever having to fear the thorns [because the intermediates are so sweet] and there is no better nurse when one is ill."

Carpenter offers a list of exceptional intermediates, including Michelangelo, Shakespeare, Marlowe, Alexander the Great and Caesar.

He cites the Greeks, briefly mentioning Cleomachus who, when preparing to leave for war, was kissed by his beloved who tenderly placed Cleomachus' helmet on his head.

He invokes Melville [a homosexual] who spoke about the "extravagant" friendships between Polynesian males, and naturally Patrocles and Achilles, Alexander and Hephaestion came up, as well as quoting a Persian poem, "Bitter and sweet is the parting kiss on the lips of a friend." Perhaps the reader would permit the intrusion of an example of Persian love: **Cyrus the Younger was going away on travels and the custom was that he kiss his relatives on the mouth. A certain lad, in love with Cyrus and wanting to be kissed too, told him that he was a distant member of his family. Cyrus said that he had noticed the lad because he never took his eyes off him. The boy blushed and said that he hadn't dared introduce himself. Cyrus said that as he was a relative, he too deserved a kiss, which he gave him. The boy said that as he too was going off on an adventure, and since Persians kissed during such times, he merited a second kiss. Cyrus laughed and bestowed it. The boy rode away but rapidly returned, his horse in a lather. "Is it not true," the boy asked, "that when one returns after a time one is received with a kiss?" "You weren't away long enough," laughed Cyrus. "How can you say that when being away from someone as** beautiful as you, for even a second, is like a year?" Cyrus again laughed and told the boy he would soon join him and that from then on he wouldn't be absent for evev a second [from my book *Greek Homosexuality*].

To continue with Carpenter and his book *The Intermediate Sex*:

Plato comes in with a quote from the *Symposium*, "I know not any greater blessing to a young man beginning life than a virtuous lover, or to the lover than a beloved youth."

Carpenter goes on to say that many intermediates marry for "ethical" and "social consideration," and form friendships with females that nonetheless are "of no avail to overcome the distaste on the part of one to sexual intercourse."

He elliptically uses expressions such as "the love in which we are dealing," and nearly never the word homosexual.

Carpenter says this of school friendships: "...between the young thing and its teacher, its importance in the educational sense can hardly be overrated." A 16-year-old says this about his tutor: "I would have died for him ten times over. My plan to meet him [to come across him casually, as it were] was that of a lad for his sweetheart, and when I saw him my heart beat so violently that it caught my breath, and I could not speak. We met in ___, and for the weeks that he stayed there I thought of nothing else-- thought of him night and day--and when he returned to London I used to write him weekly letters, veritable love-letters of many sheets in length."

"Anyone who has had experience of schoolboys knows well enough that they are capable of forming these romantic and devoted attachment," writes Carpenter.

He brings up Crete as an example of "true friendship", that receives the approbation of the boy's father. But the reality of Crete is this, another excerpt taken from my book *Greek Homosexuality*: "In Crete a boy seems to have been abducted by a lover who, in concord with the boy's friends, takes the lad into the countryside where they spend two idyllic months hunting, feasting and sexually exhausting their young bodies. The belovèd is then returned home with the symbolic gifts of military dress, an ox and a drinking cup [and whatever else the man might wish him to have, gifts the expense of which would depend on the man's resources]. Interestingly, the boy was then known by a Greek word meaning "he who stands ready," perhaps signifying Ganymede who, after being abducted by Zeus, stood ready, at the god's side, to serve him food and drink. It's interesting too to note that the boy's father was kept informed of each stage of his son's abduction and, indeed, his great wish was to have a son who would be handsome enough to attract a suitable suitor--one influential enough to give the boy a boost into the better classes, knowing full well that his boy would be the object of sexual passion, as the father had himself been as a boy."

Carpenter wrote that there was no sex education in British schools, and as a consequence a boy's desire for knowledge is filled in by his comrades: "Contraband information is smuggled in ... smut takes the place of decent explanations; unhealthy practices follow; the sacredness of sex goes its way, never to return." He states that "boys and youths must be trusted to form decent and loving friendships ... considerably more important than friendship." "Boys and youths" perpetuate the Greek ideal of boys always having older friends [lovers for the Greeks], the idea being that one instructs the other. "This was exactly the goldmine Byron fell upon. Because of his clubfoot he was mocked in college and his first year was a disaster. So the idea came, when he was in his second year, to show the new boys around and help them, warmly, to get to know the ropes. He never had a lonely night again," a quote from my book *Christ Had His John, I Have My George, The History of British Homosexuality*, a part of which recounts Byron's life.

Carpenter adds a footnote against the wisdom of sending boys 10 to 14 to boarding schools, hinting that the 15 to 18-year-olds will have their sexual will on them, which was exactly what took place.

He wrote that "the capacity of a man to devote himself to the welfare of boys and youths ought not to go wasted." And later states: "That capacity for sincere affection which causes an elder man to care so deeply for the welfare of a youth or boy is met and responded to by a similar capacity in the young thing of devotion to an elder man. This fact is not always recognized; but I have known cases of boys and even young men who would feel the most romantic attachments to quite mature men, sometimes as much as forty or fifty years of age, and only for them." This is, naturally, every older man's wet dream. One wonders at Carpenter's naivety in thinking that the boy would love a much older man for himself rather than what he was in a position to do for the boy--although, who knows?, this may have taken place.

CHAPTER SEVEN

STEPHEN SPENDER

Stephen Spender, 1909-1995, corresponded and the met Virginia Woolf in 1930. At the Woolfs he was introduced to Vanessa, Duncan, E.M. Forster, the Stracheys and other members of the Bloomsbury Set. Virginia wrote that he had an exaggerated sense of his talents, "a young man who thinks himself the greatest poet of all time." In her diary she added that he had "the makings of a long-winded bore" and was "married to a Sergeant of the Guards", his lover at the time, Guardsman Tony Hyndmen. In addition to Virginia, both Spender and Tony spent a great deal of time with

Forster and his lover ex-policeman Bob Buckingham.

Spender had sent Virginia Woolf some of his poems when he was 21 [1930], an undergraduate at Oxford. He also sent poems to Virginia's lover Vita Sackville-West with whom he corresponded for years. Stephen was a Bloomsbury boy in and of himself, as he was sex crazy, his taste for teenage boys insatiable [even his closest friend, W.H. Auden, criticized him for bedding so many], and would eventually marry, twice, a bisexuality practiced by the Set, something Virginia was highly attuned to, given her affairs with women, although she never cared for Spender's first wife Inez.

Stephen had had prep-school lovers and lovers at Oxford (2), but it was Berlin that liberated his sexuality, Berlin that Duncan Grant had discovered with Franzi von Haas. Because Berlin represented the wildest form of homosexual promiscuity known to the world since the Romans, and many of the members of the Bloomsbury Set made their way there at some time during their lives, we will now go to Berlin in the company of Spender and Spender's two inseparable friends, Christopher Isherwood and Auden.

What is amazing in the history of love among males was that after the Renaissance there followed an age darker than the Middle Ages which had preceded the Renaissance. Love between males during the Renaissance could be punished by death, but in reality under Lorenzo *Il Magnifico* de' Medici one got off easily because everyone was doing it, sharing, at some point in their lives, an orgasm with another male. As girls were worth their weight in gold thanks to advantageous marriages that would enrich their husbands, they were kept locked away. Unlike a boy who could offer himself to a hundred passing hands or mouths or anuses and still claim innocence, a girl had one chance, after which the fruit was eternally spoiled.

After the Renaissance we stepped back into the dark, where lads, in the 1800s, could not comprehend their attraction to other lads, those they saw swimming in rivers and lakes, naked and so beautiful the boys dreaming of them inundated their own bellies in equally wondrous rivers and lakes. Till then, men were thought [by some] to have become homosexual because they were so insatiable sexually that they simply turned to men as an alternative to women who now bored them. Sexuality was malleable, and one could alter it at will. To keep boys on the right track laws were harsh, although thankfully the death penalty had been dropped, except, in one of life's never-ending paradoxes, in Berlin--until 1868. It was felt that men who cared for other men were in reality women trapped in a man's body, which would not only account for their searching out other men, but would account too for those who were effeminate. The woman within was seeking an outlet for her femininity.

Men who were lucky, mostly educated men who emigrated to Berlin, could find sexual satisfaction in the garrison city of 400,000 where soldiers padded their pay by selling themselves, and that for generations. The unlucky ones, the vast majority, may have felt that they and their sexuality were alone in the world, that no others shared their dreams and lust. These would live and die alone. Following the French Revolution laws against sodomy were abolished in France in 1791. Under French influence they were abolished also in Spain, Belgium, the Netherlands and Italy. Certain parts of Germany followed. In Bavaria, for example, only those who raped other men or who had sex with boys under 12 were prosecuted. But in all parts of Germany men could be imprisoned if they did something against public decency. The population of Berlin exploded, from the 400,000 to 4 million in 1920. Berlin went from a city of open sewers to the first city ever electrified, with, in 1800, electric streetcars and lighting. It went from a city of open sewers to one of public toilets and baths, from the filthiest to the cleanest city in the world, infinitely more hygienic than London, Paris and New York. At the end of the 1400s in Florence the Office of the Night was formed to put an end to sodomy. The penalty was death but everyone got off lightly, except those who forced children to have sex. In 1885 Berlin established the Department of Homosexuals, proof of the growing number of gays. The police collected information and mug shots of homosexuals, and encouraged doctors and educators to study Berlin's unique sexual subculture, thanks to which reams of information concerning the sexuality of the times have come to us. In 1896 the name of the Department of Homosexuals was changed to Department of Homosexuals and Blackmailers. More money could be gained by pimps putting 14-year-old boys on the streets and then blackmailing the clients. In 1902 Friedrich Alfred Krupp, the Cannon King, committed suicide when blackmail led to the publication of his preference for Italian boys. For such a rich, powerful man to end his own life so young spoke volumes about being branded a homosexual, about the prevalence of blackmail and about the availability of underage lads. The department store magnate Hermann Israel killed himself on his yacht at age 40 when his companion blackmailed him. Before dying Israel turned the boy's threatening letters over to the police. The lad was sentenced to two months imprisonment. Victims of blackmail numbered in the hundreds, two of whom were well-known jurists, one who shot his blackmailer when he literally didn't have a cent left to pay him off. In 1902 a 28-year-old ophthalmologist committed suicide when his card was found in a boy's jacket and the ophthalmologist was threatened with a trial. At the time, it was established that a third of Berlin's homosexuals were being blackmailed. But as Berlin's reputation for male prostitution bloomed, johns from all over Europe flocked to the world's greatest center of boys.

Although boy whorehouses would number in the hundreds in pre-W.W. I years, the beginnings in the very early 1900s were rudimentary, where everyone from a club owner to a tobacconist could use a backroom for financial gain, recruiting hustlers and unemployed boys from off the streets. Any man could have a room and rent out his boys, as pimps have since the beginning of time. And as the boys were often twelve to fifteen, their suitors could be either blackmailed or robbed while busy with their young prey. Any schoolboy or shop boy, any servant or thief, sailor or soldier, could round off monthly earnings by playing innocent or butch or changing into drag. Rich men like Friedrich Alfred Krupp, as stated, were openly blackmailed, or writers would threaten to publish tell-all books if they didn't pay up. Some hustlers trailed likely johns and then, catching hold of them, accused them of soliciting and threatened to call the police.

What happened next was pretty much inexplicable to rationalists. As clubs gained in number so did those who took advantage of johns, robbing and blackmailing them. More and more targets were out-of-town Germans [city dwellers became streetwise], many well-off merchants and industrialists. This in turn inspired more boys to go to Berlin, which in turn drew still more men seeking youths. Soon the British came, followed by Americans. Those who sought and bought sex returned home to flaunt the merits of Berlin's boys, often hung, often highly-sexed lads who, because of their growing numbers, cost less and less. The minority of men robbed and otherwise extorted turned more and more to the police who had such complete files on the boys, largely thanks to the effective Chief of Police Leopold von Meerscheidt-Hüllessem, that the lads were often apprehended and the stolen goods retrieved. This made great copy for newspapers, thanks to which more and more foreigners learned about Berlin's boys. More rent and johns flocked to the new gay oasis, in [small] part responsible for its population exploding to 4 million, including [according to one estimate] a pre-W.W. II total of 170 boy bordellos. More than an oasis, Berlin became an earthly heaven because every variation of sex was represented, because beer and liquor flowed, and because of hugely successful floorshows, as seen in Isherwood's *Cabaret*.

That said, many German boys practiced sports that kept their bodies trim, and naked sunbathing took place around lakes, along rivers and even in public swimming pools, thanks to which the boys were beautifully tanned. Many foreign lads, especially the English, the opposite of this, hesitated to denude themselves. Yet sex at the time was so free that Stephen Spender, at first unwilling to expose his physique, soon found himself at home in Berlin, and as far as love was concerned, ''all one had to do was undress'', Spender concluded. German boys tended to be masculine, they liked to exercise and they liked to show off their toned bodies. Their smiles were often ravaging, they enjoyed roughhousing, and sexually were highly experienced. Compared to the English they were animals, studs to British boarding-school lads used to lying on their stomachs in wait of the thrill of penetration, something many boys beg for. Of his intimate friend Pieps, Spender's best friend Auden said, ''I like sex and Pieps likes money. It's a good exchange.''

Kiosks were literally flooded with dozens of publications, and the kiosk owners didn't hesitate to have some pinned open, showing nude males. In 1930 Berlin had 280,000 tourists a year, among which were 40,000 Americans. There were believed to have been 50,000 rent-boys, all out for money to live on or pocket change, 1/3rd were believed to have been heterosexual. And they were cheap, especially soldiers and sailors going for 50 pfennig. Thomas Mann discovered Berlin at age 17. Christopher Isherwood refused to spend more than 10 marks, dinner and a few drinks for his boys [although this was outrageously overpaying], W.H. Auden, in his diary, detailed his sexual encounters, and the architect Philip Johnson claimed to have learned German through the horizontal method.

Auden, Spender and Isherwood

Sex was tame in some high-class clubs [although no-holds-barred was the rule in boy whorehouses]. At the urinals boys flashed their wares, and at tables boys allowed johns to put their hands through their pockets, which had been cut away inside to allow them to grasp the lads' dicks. Lederhosen were popular in the butch places Isherwood frequented, showing off boys' suntanned thighs. Isherwood was said to have had 500 during the time he was there, from 1929 to 1933. The beautiful boys were in private clubs and in private hands, wealthy hands, hands that could offer far more than Isherwood's ten marks, even if ten marks were extremely generous for what was available. The boys who went with Isherwood thought he was fabulously rich because they were fabulously lacking in the attributes that would place them in an entirely different class. That said, Isherwood wrote that there were so many postulants that he always found a handsome lad for the night.

Boys of quality in pre-W.W. I Berlin were in private hands, not Stephen Spender's.

Then, as today, coke was ubiquitous, except that it had just been invented, by Albert Niemann, and was not only fully accepted, it was recommended by Freud to his patients. Klaus Mann preferred heroine but also took cocaine, said to circulate like cigarettes, and everyone was into other drugs, like morphine and opium. After using coke one writer said, ''I felt exhilarated, strong and capable of going on without tiredness.'' Some doctors and researchers believed that men became homosexual when using cocaine, that the drug was the cause, while most believed that coke simply lessened inhibitions, which liberated men with latent homosexuality or bisexuality to free themselves from self-imposed restraints. Cocaine helped one become more sociable and less shy.

Lederhosen provided immediate and all-inclusive access.

Due to English law that had seen a veritable genius like Oscar Wilde sent to prison (4), the English couldn't write freely about homosexuality, and even Byron's poetic references to homosexual love come out as gibberish, so vague are the allusions. An example of this is Shelley, who is known to have written the best description of orgasm ever, according to some, a perfect example of Victorian clarity:

> The Serchio, twisting forth
> Between the marble barriers which it clove
> At Ripafratta, leads through the dread chasm
> The wave that died the death which lovers love,
> Living in what it sought; as if this spasm
> Had not yet passed, the toppling mountains cling,
> But the clear stream in full enthusiasm
> Pours itself on the plain.

Spender therefore appreciated the freedoms in Germany, which had existed since Frederick the Great gave Voltaire the permission to publish a book that revealed Frederick's homosexual adventures (10). The press in Paris was also free, but writers like Gide and Montherlant didn't dare expose themselves until the end of their lives, and Proust gave female identities to his male lovers [so afraid were they of losing their readers] (11). Spender had also deeply appreciated German boys, so unlike the English--milquetoast, anemic, asthmatic sissies with poor eyesight and varicose veins, most of whom, including Isherwood, Auden and Spender himself, could not get into the war because of their poor physical condition, boys who sexually preferred to spread out over a bed and passively wait to be taken. [Of course, many English lads are exquisite, Brooke, Duncan Grant, the Davies brother, Mark Gertler, Louis Mountbatten (4) and Byron are examples, Byron during those brief periods when he was not overweight].

Concerning love between boys and girls, he made this silly comment: "I find boys much more attractive, in fact I am much more than usually susceptible, but erotically I find the actual sexual act with women more satisfactory, more terrible, more disgusting and, in fact, more everything." But he compensated by stating, "Whatever happens, I shall never be alone. I shall always have a boy, a railway fare, or a revolution."

Spender was inspired by social protests, full-heartedly in favor of the advance of the under-classes, and went to Spain during the Spanish Civil War to do what he could for the Republicans, outside of fighting, while his lover Tony Hyndman joined the International Brigade. The loss of the Republicans was a terrible setback for Spain, which even today has remnants of the disaster in maintaining royalty put in place by Franco. Back in England he married twice and joined the Communist Party despite the Molotov-Ribbentrop Pact between Nazi Germany and the Russia of Stalin. He cofounded *Horizon* and *Encounter*, both literary magazines. He became Poet Laureate Consultant in Poetry to the United States Library of Congress, professor and then Professor Emeritus at University College,

London. He was knighted in 1983 and died of a heart attack in 1995, at age 86.

CHAPTER EIGHT

MAYNARD KEYNES

At this very moment, somewhere in the world, economists and philosophers have the name of John Maynard Keynes, 1883-1946, on their lips, perhaps furiously in favor of his ideas, perhaps furiously against, but all are as respectful as before an ancient god. Among the Bloomsbury Setters, he is by far the shining light, and even the name of Virginia Woolf is remembered, today, if the public is asked, for the play by Albee *Who's Afraid of Virginia Woolf?* Roger Fry did a great deal to ensure the reputation of Bloomsbury members, especially that of Duncan Grant, as well as seeing to their creature comforts, but it was Keynes who stepped in when the power of the government, legal advice, guarantees for loans, help in the purchase of homes and land, were required. He provided Duncan Grant with an annuity, and most certainly aided others in need, backstage, out of love and humanism. We have every reason to get to know this truly exceptional human being.

Free markets today are an accepted fact, which, along with flexible employer-employee relations, provide full employment, something which the present president of France is striving to push through, now, in 2017, against a people who are not only stodgy, but basically impossible to reform, the consequence being that France has the highest unemployment in the entire euro zone. It was Keynes who was the first to spearhead, in the 1930s, the then-revolutionary idea of free markets. Keynes fought for virile intervention in fiscal and monetary policies, thanks to which the disaster of 1929 came to an end, as well as the world financial crises of 2007-2008.

In 1990 TIME magazine wrote, ''his radical idea that governments should spend money they don't have may have saved capitalism.''

Keynes made the cover of TIME on the 31st of December 1965. TIME wrote, ''We are all Keynesians now.''

Keynes was born in Cambridge, Cambridgeshire, to upper-middle-class parents, his father an economist and lecturer at Cambridge, his mother a social reformer, the perfect storm in the creation of this humanist genius. His brother became a surgeon, his sister married a Nobel Prize-winning physiologist. Lovingly raised, all three children never strayed far from home and the care of both parents.

Keynes was damned with poor health but compensated with brilliance in mathematics, the classics and history, which saw him into Eton with a scholarship, Eton where he met his first love, Dan Macmillan, older brother of Prime Minister Harold [another early lover was Dillwyn "Dilly" Knox, who was also Lytton Strachey's lover, Strachey who said of Keynes: he treated "his love affairs statistically", and who wrote this poem about Keynes: Both penetrating and polite/A liberal and a sodomite/An atheist and a statistician/A man of sense, without ambition/A man of business, without bustle/A follower of Moore and Russell/One who, in fact, in every way/Combined the features of the day].

In 1902 Keynes went to King's College, Cambridge, thanks to another scholarship, this one in mathematics, even though the true love of his life was philosophy and history. He was an active member of the Apostles, as covered in their chapter, as well as one of the original members of the Bloomsbury Set. His family love instilled an eternal optimism in Keynes, self-confidence and the belief that man could do good and that governments could and must come to the aid of its citizens. He began publishing his first articles on economics in 1909, at age 26, and in 1911 became editor of *The Economic Journal*. He accepted a government position in the Treasury in 1915 and gave lectures. At Versailles, at the end of the First World War, he fought to prevent the allies' demands for German compensation that he knew would destroy the German people, a fight he lost, which led, first, to his resignation from the Treasury and, second, W.W. II. [Historian Stephen Schuker wrote that Keynes became an informal reparations advisor to the German government and supported hyperinflation on political grounds, all of which made him *persona non grata* in Britain until the Second World War.]

In 1919 he became chairman of the British Bank of Northern Commerce in exchange for working one morning per week, at a salary of £2,000, £95,000 today, or £8,000 per month]. Keynes wrote that the purpose of work was to provide leisure, and felt that everyone should work fewer hours and have longer vacations.

At the height of the Great Depression he wrote *The Means to Prosperity*, based on the need for government public spending, a copy of which went to Franklin Roosevelt, and Keynesian became the adjective applied to all new economic ideas. Without government intervention to increase expenditures, insisted Keynes, low employment would continue.

Keynes suffered a first heart attack in 1937 at age 54.

His contribution to W.W. II came in his 1940 book *How to Pay for the War* in which he recommended higher taxation, compulsory savings [the money thereby lent to the government], and the dampening of domestic demand, which would lead to less inflation, and industrial production would be diverted to the war effort and not into domestic households. After the war the money the public had stashed away in government bonds and banks would serve to insure an economic boom, which is precisely what took place. Keynes was given a seat as one of the directors of the Bank of England, as well as a hereditary peerage that came with another seat, this one in the House of Lords. At Bretton Woods Keynes argued for a world currency, the bancor, and a world central bank, ideas overruled by Americans, although the International Monetary Fund was established as a compromise. Keynes's plans were always in support of poor countries, what he called "the brotherhood of man". The 2007-2008 crises spurred the *Financial Times* to write, "the sudden resurgence of Keynesian policy is a stunning reversal of the orthodoxy of the past several decades." Incredibly, in 2009 the government of the People's Bank of China came out in favor of Keynes's idea for a world bank and a centrally managed global reserve currency, the bancor. If this could not be enacted, maintained the Chinese, greater funds should be given to the IMF for distribution, which was done in 2009 with a deposit of $250 billion, a vital step in the slow recovery that has continued up to this writing, 2017. After Keynes's death economist Friedrich Hayek wrote, "He was the really only great man I knew, and for whom I had unbounded admiration. The world will be a very much poorer place without him." And it's true that Keynes's intelligence and charm could seduce everyone, from presidents to ministers to the hotel bellboys Keynes so greatly desired, boys lucky to have the company of this gentle, certainly loving man.

Keynes's earliest loves were, besides Dilly Knox and Daniel Macmillan, Lytton Strachey, his brother James, Duncan Grant, Arthur Hobhouse [Hobby], and Charles Fay, a freshman at King's College who introduced Keynes into the dregs of Soho where guardsmen could be found and had for half a crown. During the first part of his life his liaisons were exclusively with men, but in 1906, at age 23, he claimed he liked the girl Ray Costelloe [who later married Lytton's brother Oliver] and wrote in his diary: "I have fallen in love with Ray a little bit, but as she isn't male I haven't been able to think of any suitable steps to take."

Keynes was the first to criticize his looks, stating, "Yes, I have a clever head, a weak character, an affectionate disposition, and a repulsive appearance." To Lytton Strachey he wrote, "I have always suffered from a most unalterable obsession that I am so physically repulsive that I have no business to hurl my body at anyone else's.''

As said, thanks to his parents he had nonetheless an extremely positive view on life, and countered his homeliness with flirtatious advances that were never vulgar, just extremely friendly, and he loved to demonstrate that friendliness with physical contact, not unlike the American president Lyndon Johnson much later, who couldn't keep his hands off people, so eager was he to share his fondness, be they male or female.

Keynes was circumcised, the reason being the Masturbation Panic described in detail in the last chapter of this book. The foreskin and its movement up and down the glans was blamed for drawing a boy's attention to his penis, leading to masturbation and the mental and physical illnesses that followed. Keynes went under the knife at age 8, an incredibly painful procedure, the agony lasting for weeks. Some doctors at the time suggested the operation be done without anesthetic, as the boy would then identify the pain as a punishment for touching the penis. When Keynes was 11 his father had the pockets of his overcoat sewn up so he couldn't fondle himself [his father confided to his diary], and most probably those of his trousers too. Richard Davenport-Hines, in his *The Seven Lives of John Maynard Keynes,* states that a politician, Lord Hailsham, still remembered the pain 70 years later, the blood ''and my sense of betrayal by the adult world''. [W.H. Auden was circumcised at age 7, after which he became erotically captivated by boys who had foreskins, as was the pornography star Al Parker, an obsession extensively discussed in my book *Phallus.*]

Keynes's obsession with numbers pushed him to note everything. From May 1908 to February 1909, he wrote in his diary, he had 61 sexual encounters, mainly with Duncan Grant and with both Strachey brothers, Lytton and James. From February 1909 to February 1910 he had 65 encounters; 26 from February 1910 to February 1911, and 39 from February 1911 to February 1912. His diaries were heavily encoded but the following items have been deciphered: He wrote of having sex with ''a 16-year-old under Etna'' and ''the liftboy of Vauxhall''. In 1911 he had 16 C's, 4 A's and 5 W's. Encoders guess the A's were ass-contacts, the C's cocksucking and the W's wanks [jerking off] with boys/men. The baths and saunas were the easiest places to find contacts, and Keynes knew all the parks, hotels and sites where guardsmen earned extra cash. As sodomy was punishable by imprisonment, under the same law that had seen Oscar Wilde sent away, guardsmen had to be careful. When one of Keynes's favorites was found out and was dismissed from service, he took cyanide, being, apparently, *far* from the exception. The 2008 edition of *The Atlantic* stated that the compulsion to calculate everything began in childhood, when he counted and remembered the number of steps leading up to the houses on the street where he lived, as well as detailed records of his expenses and his golf scores [and his sexual encounters]. In his diaries he gave the initials of the men he was bedding, GLS for Lytton Strachey, DG for Grant and nicknames, Tressider for the King's college Provost J.T. Sheppard. What went on within the Bloomsbury Set was described by Keynes's biographer Robert Skidelsky as a "sexual merry-to-round". At the time, claim his friends, he was as obsessed with whom he would share an orgasm as he was later with economic affairs or philosophy. Keynes wrote this about the Bloomsbury Set, "We repudiated general rules. We repudiated customary morals, conventions and traditional wisdom. We were, in the strict sense of the term, immoralists." For Keynes self-denial was bad, self-indulgence good [which was the undercurrent of his financial policy too]. "After all," he wrote, "in the long run we're all dead."

From 1909 to 1914 Keynes made love to St George Nelson, a model he'd met posing for Duncan. He paid for Nelson's sex with female prostitutes and participated in threesomes, Nelson, another boy Keynes would pick up in the street and a girl, careful to be only in skin contract with the boys. Alas, Nelson was killed on the Western Front in 1916. Keynes looked for boys on streets favored by homosexuals, but preferred Cambridge boys and the discretion of Cambridge bedrooms, although the boys were mostly effeminate. George Mallory, on the other hands, sought strong, strapping lads, skirting scandal when they refused his advances, although when they didn't, the sex was wonderfully virile. Keynes often had sex with Frankie Birrell, David Garnett's pal, an undergraduate then at King's College, six years younger than Keynes, although effeminate too. Keynes got Frankie a job as a theater critic for the *Nation*, as he had found work in the theater for St George Nelson. Keynes *always* came through for his lovers.

Keynes allowed Lytton to have a look at his diaries, those that covered 1909 to 1911, which spurned Lytton to dub him an "iron copulating machine". Keynes even participated in the research done by Berlin sexologist Magnus Hirschfeld for his treatise *Die Homosexualität*, 1913 (10), by filling in a questionnaire.

Wartime was amazingly fruitful in homosexual encounters, a combination of London blackouts and boys aware that they might soon be killed in combat and during blitzes, which freed their libidos. It was suspected that the Germans had turned loose beautiful boys to entrap men like Keynes, already high in government, his potential as ministerial material known to be unlimited, as were the possibilities of blackmail.

Davenport-Hines suggests that it was because Keynes was surrounded by homosexuals settling down with women or marrying them, as was the case with Duncan and Vanessa, and Lytton with Dora Carrington. He heard again and again how marriage was "such a comfort" and "so convenient" [no spunk to clean up from a lover's belly, as David Garnett had so delicately put it]. Another lover, Sidney Russell-Cooke, wrote him that he too was planning to marry, his choice the only child of the captain of the *Titanic*. Sidney's best man was a "pansy", wrote a friend, and Sidney himself described his bride in a letter to Keynes, brought to us by Davenport-Hines: "She's certainly lovely, reasonably intelligent, some money [more in prospect], damn randy." They would have two children, before Sidney killed himself with a shotgun. Finally, just before his marriage Keynes had an affair with Sebastian Sprott, an Apostle.

Keynes married Lydia Lopokova in 1925, Lopokova a ballerina in Diaghilev's Ballets Russes in 1925, he age 47, which chilled the members of the Bloomsbury Set [a perplexing outcome because most of them wound up marrying, and even Duncan Grant lived with Vanessa Bell for 40 years, a marriage in all but name]. Keynes told Lytton Strachey that he had found the combination of beauty and sex in only one person, Duncan Grant. Keynes's marriage brought no children, although Lydia did miscarry in 1927. She was intelligent, and E.M. Forster wrote, "How we all used to underestimate her." As for the marriage, her biographer described her sex life with Keynes as all fingers and mouth.

At Keynes's passing, in 1946, he was worth £500,000 [£20 million today], and he possessed the works of Picasso, Degas, Cézanne, Modigliani, Braque and Seurat. He died of a heart attack at age 62.

CHAPTER NINE

LYTTON STRACHEY
From age 13 to age 37

Giles Lytton Strachey, born in 1880--the eleventh of thirteen children, three who died during their infancy--was called Giles by the family, although the name Lytton would soon impose itself. As his parentage has already been covered, we will begin Lytton's story at his entry in Abbotsholme School in 1893, at age 13. The school had been founded only four years previously by Dr Cecil Reddie, open to boys 11 to 18. There were 40 students at the time, some of whom worshipped Reddie, most others, including the staff, were in dire fear of him. Reddie was a progressionist, and the purpose of his school was the production of boys with wide-ranging skills, boys cultured and athletic. The curriculum was amazingly varied, and precise to the minute: the boys were up at 5 to 7, bathed in cold water, fell out on the parade ground for military-like drill and exercises with dumb-bells, 20 minutes at chapel and then classes, very short at 40 minutes [compared to other schools], with a preference for German and French rather than Greek and Latin [an immense innovation]. Lunch was followed by drawing, carpentry, basket weaving and bee-culture, boot making and tailoring, and even instruction in how to make butter. Planting, harvesting and the cleaning of the cowshed where part of the agenda, with tea at 6 followed by 30 free minutes. Glee-singing came next, after which visits from outsiders were encouraged, met by the students who conducted themselves "in adult fashion", states Michael Holroyd in his remarkable *Lytton Strachey*, 1994, who provided the above school curriculum. Bedtime came at 8:50.

Lytton acquired his love of literature from his mother who was in advance of her times, smoking even American cigarettes, but she deliberately took second place to her husband, as was expected. The Stracheys were well-off, enough to have a butler and servants, but a house with so many children and only one toilet must have been a challenge. Literature was studied at Abbotsholme, although because Reddie didn't favor composition Lytton didn't receive the encouragement Duncan Grant would later benefit from in his school. He took part in school plays, accorded the role of women. He participated in sports and those who saw him naked in the baths noticed he was circumcised and therefore different from the other boys, which didn't seem to bother him [although he may have realized, later, that circumcision destroyed the natural beauty of the instrument so vital in a man's life, in addition to depriving him of the masturbatory pleasures due to the natural lubrication offered by the foreskin (see my book *Phallus*)]. Circumcision was conducted massively after the Masturbation Panic, detailed in the last chapter, because it was believed that the movement of the foreskin over the glans drew a boy's attention to his penis, leading to masturbation and the physical disabilities and mental illness it caused.

The difference in ages at the school, from 11 to 18, encouraged bullying, and Lytton wrote, "At school I used to weep ... due to the bitter unkindness and vile brutality," a quote from Holroyd. The brutality came naturally to many boys, that some allayed through boxing, a highly admired sport. Underlining it all was sexual domination over the younger lads, the bigger, more athletic students having first choice of the most handsome juniors. Sex was taken very seriously, and those that didn't come willingly could be forced. When a new pretty face came along the former favorite was sent off to service an older boy's friends, before whom he was expected to bend over and drop his pants, no foreplay, nor lubrication other than spit. Earlier I gave this quote from J.A. Symonds that I would like to repeat: "The talk in the dormitories and studies was of the grossest character, with repulsive scenes of onanism, mutual masturbation and obscene orgies of naked boys in bed together. There was no refinement, just animal lust" (2). Lytton was not an attractive boy, and would never know the intense passion that took place nightly in the beds of handsome lads and school athletes. Throughout his life he would gain what he wanted by bombarding those he lusted for with letters and invitations to dinners and trips throughout England and abroad, his hope being to get the boy to himself, the time to work his charm. In the end, he would have them all, mostly for short periods, an exception being the extremely good-looking Mark Gertler who stayed out of his way from the moment Lytton made his intentions clear. The degree of Gertler's heterosexuality was a particularity for the times, when most lads were omnisexual to a high degree. Even Duncan's last true love, Paul Roche, who proclaimed loud and clear his devotion to women, let Duncan have his way with him [although banning all attempts at sodomy], and he would occasionally return from the baths or lakes or swimming pools for a secluded hour with a boy he had met there. [Even Clive Bell, who had countless mistresses, jumped at the occasion to sleep with Duncan Grant]. Only girls were attracted to Lytton, but then girls have another agenda, whereas boys mostly just want to conclude, and then move on to the next boy.

Dr Reddie wrote Lytton's father to say how well Lytton was doing in math, English, Latin, Greek and French, and Lytton was taking in the numerous other activities offered by the school, editing the school magazine, going on nature expeditions, playing cricket and "performing the most brilliant feats" when skating, he modestly informed his mother. He was made head of house at age 15, which wouldn't have been the case had he been unpopular.

Lytton's mother was agnostic, and Lytton followed suit. He discovered and adored Gibbon, second only to his love of Plato's *Symposium* (5), and he worshiped Alcibiades (12), for whom many a boy has succumbed from a distance of 2,000 years.

He was remarkably aware of the nature of boys, as when he wrote, concerning two lads that he adored from afar, "both had that curious softness which some boys of about seventeen seem to be able to mingle with their brutality". About his own seventeenth birthday he wrote to his mother, "I am quite appalled by my great age", an awareness of the passage of time unheard of in one so young.

He entered Trinity, Cambridge, in 1899. He must have been strange in appearance because one student said it was as if he'd come from "a different civilization". His body was ungainly, he was shortsighted and he had "the breathless squeak of an asthmatic rabbit", added painter and writer Graham Robertson. Holroyd says it best: "here was a new animal in their midst, alien yet inoffensive, whom it was not easy to accept and impossible to ignore." The first person he became friends with was Clive Bell. He then met Maynard Keynes who described him as "a gay and amiable dog". Thoby Stephen followed, of huge importance because he introduced Lytton into the Stephen family, consisting of Duncan's adored Adrian, along with Vanessa and Virginia and Virginia's future husband

Leonard Woolf, with whom Lytton would remain a lifelong friend. Lytton fell head over heels for Thoby, about whom he wrote, ''Don't you think that if God had to justify the existence of the world, it would be done if he were to produce the Goth?'', the nickname for Thoby because of his ''barbaric splendor,'' said Lytton.

Julian Thoby Stephen, the Goth [due to his height of over six feet and athletic build], was the brother of Vanessa Bell, Virginia Woolf and Adrian Stephen. He is said to have started the Bloomsbury Set by inaugurating the Set's Thursday evening gatherings. Alas, he died of typhoid in Greece at age 26. Vanessa named her first child Julian, in his memory. Julian was sincerely and deeply loved by everyone who had come into contact with him.

Lytton interspersed his studies with visits to both France and Italy, two safe havens that would be second homes to the Bloomsbury Set throughout all their lives, with a few excursions to America. He was befriended by G.E. Moore, Bertrand Russell and E.M. Forster, all of whom would have various secondary roles to play during his lifetime.

He was elected to the Apostles in 1902, a moment of jubilation and the promise of limitless casual sex, for when he eventually became an angel he had a word in the choice of embryos, and later he would direct the Apostles with Keynes, a situation both were keen to exploit. Leonard Woolf was elected the same year as Lytton, and perfectly summed up the group in this quote brought to us by Holroyd: ''Our common bond has been a common intellectual taste, common studies, common literary aspirations, and we have all felt, I suppose, the support of mutual regard and perhaps some mutual flattery. We soon grew, as such youth coteries generally do, into immense self-conceit. We began to think we had a mission to enlighten the world upon things intellectual and spiritual.''

Lytton met and mated with John Sheppard, whom he called ''my first, last, and only Frank''. They remained together for two years, and in addition to sharing literary and theatrical tastes, they were both gaga over Thoby Stephen. A major difference between Lytton and Sheppard reveals volumes concerning Lytton. Sheppard liked everyone, despite their class, while Lytton ridiculed Sheppard's forays into the lower classes, what Lytton called his intellectual inferiors, and in fact turned his back on anyone who was not an Apostle. They finally separated, Lytton writing to Leonard Woolf, "I'm fairly bored with him, and as frigid as if he were a lovely young lady," a quote from Holroyd that, again, speaks volumes about the nature of Lytton Strachey [the only enigma being how the affair went on so long].

Maynard Keynes became an Apostle in 1903. Keynes would largely replace Leonard Woolf as Lytton's confident, even if Lytton found Keynes "stiff and stern", while Bertrand Russell said that Keynes's mind "was the sharpest and clearest I have ever known". Both Lytton and Keynes shared poor health, both were unattractive, both intellectual and intellectually curious, both homosexual [the reason, in Keynes's case, his later marriage raised outraged eyebrows], and both fell deeply in love with the same boy, the boy everyone seemed to want, Arthur Lawrence Hobhouse, lovingly called Hobby or Hobber. Hobby became an Apostle in 1905 and Keynes immediately laid claim to him, Hobby becoming the first real love of Keynes's life. Hobby told James Strachey that he felt a "revulsion", whether for Keynes or for the sexual act with Keynes is not known, although it would seem that Hobby may have been in the Ravel class of lovers (1), undersexed or perhaps lacking a sufficient percentage of homosexuality to be lustful, or maybe he had been attracted by Keynes's brilliant mind and turned off by his body. Lytton would later get his chance to closely worship Hobby's body, as would Duncan and nearly everyone else, none of whom came away sexually fulfilled.

Perhaps to reestablish good relations with Lytton, Keynes introduced him to Bernard Swithinbank, Keynes's Eton lover, whom Lytton found a suitable replacement for Hobby. The letter Bernard wrote Keynes after having tea with Lytton for the first time is incredibly revealing as to Lytton's attraction to boys: "When I left him I was in a condition. Lord, lord. I didn't know one could have such affection without lust. But there it is. He's unique--exquisite. I only know one other work of the Creator equally beautiful as an esthetic whole--the Goth [Thoby Stephen]." "Exquisite" would often be the word chosen to describe Lytton.

Swithinbank was soon replaced by someone Lytton had known over the years, his young cousin Duncan Grant. Lytton was now 25 and wrote to Duncan: "You don't know what it is to be twenty-five, dejected, uncouth, unsuccessful--you don't know how humble and wretched and lonely I sometimes feel." Yet he was partially to blame, as he too fell in and out of love as often as he himself had been rejected. And he was right to feel the pressure of age, as he would be dead when only 52.

James Strachey joined the Apostle in 1906 and Rupert Brooke two years later. Pronounced exquisite in beauty, Brooke had to keep his popularity with the boys from his parents, such was their sexual passion and willingness to overtly show it. Brooke bathed naked with Virginia Woolf and Lytton, and came out of the water with a full erection that turned off Virginia, while Lytton wrote, "absolutely beautiful!"

Lytton had the gift of maintaining lovers as friends throughout his entire life, and years and years later we find him visiting or dining or having tea with this or that former flame.

Lytton truly wanted love, affection and a hand-in-hand march to artistic success with Duncan. For Lytton, Duncan was not a boy passing through. He wrote Keynes, "He sees everything ... and is probably better than us. When I hear people talking about him I'm filled with secret pride." [I know how Lytton felt, as I had once been madly in love with a German actor who was starring in a play. When he came on stage shirtless, the audience of men and women audibly gasped at the sight of his beauty. Yet is was I--I felt bursting with pride--who would sleep in his arms that night (13).]

Holroyd strikes the nail on the head when he wrote that Duncan was "fond" of Lytton, and it was this lack of true love that made Lytton overly possessive, stifling the boy. Duncan was at the age when he was at his most beautiful, when he attracted great numbers of admirers, the age at which his body craved caresses, meaning there was no question of his limiting himself to one person. Holroyd states that Lytton despised himself, and that he would automatically think less of someone who could show him love, and so, to the contrary, the more Duncan pulled away, the more Lytton worshipped him. Were Duncan to love him, the reasoning went, Lytton would no longer respect nor love him. Presumably, with the later successes of his books, Lytton would regain self-respect, something I personally disbelieve. An ingrained lack of self-love is like a child physically abused, sexually or through beatings: he never gets over it, although he can become an expert at masking it. "The whole world stinks in my nostrils" Lytton wrote Keynes in 1906, a year after he first bedded Duncan.

Offered a gift of money for his 21st birthday, Duncan went to Paris to study art, where he came upon Hobby and wrote to Lytton, "I suppose I should blurt it out as fast as possible. Hobhouse as you know has been staying here and I have fallen in love with him and he with me." Lytton wrote Keynes, "I'm still gasping". Lytton went to Paris the moment Hobby left. Duncan visited him at his hotel, sat at the foot of his bed, and they talked. Just talked.

Thoby the Goth died in Greece and Lytton wrote to Keynes, "I am stunned. The loss is too great, and seems to have taken what is best in life. Leonard Woolf wrote to Lytton, "I am overwhelmed, crushed ... he was an anchor. He was above everyone in his nobility."

Lytton began work as a journalist, doing reviews, writing Keynes: "Reviews dribble from [my pen] somewhat in the manner of Hobber's semen." To which Keynes wrote back, congratulating him on his journalistic style [!]. Speaking of Hobby, Lytton was still madly in love with him, as he was with Duncan, acquiescing to Duncan's every caprice, and even after a dinner he wrote to the boy apologizing for anything untoward he may have said. He was totally under Duncan's boot, perhaps a first step on his way to later sadomasochism with others, which included crucifixions.

In 1907 Lytton met Angelica Homere, one of the many women who would desire Lytton's love, as he desired Duncan's, women who would follow him even after confirmation of his homosexuality, one who would eventually kill herself for him, while Lytton had not only written "I'm as frigid as if he were a lovely young lady", but Holroyd wrote that Lytton repeatedly wished he had been born a lady himself. Yet it was with women that he spent his time, a holiday in Menton in the company of extremely old ones, and he wrote Duncan, studying art in Paris, that during "the intervals of these orgies"--his lunches and dinners with London hostesses, all women of a certain age--he was working on his book reviews. Although Cambridge was going through a golden age of homosexuality, he on the outside looking in, it was in the company of those he wished to be but not bed, women, that Lytton spent his time.

His luck at finding work was going infinitely better than his love life, as he was hired by the *Spectator* and the *New Quarterly* to do book reviews and write articles, salaries that would make him financially independent. As related earlier, Lytton never gave up a friendship, and this at times paid off sexually as when he spent some quality time with Duncan in 1907, saw and slept with Swithinbank again, although they all lost Hobby, whose mother came across a letter sent to him, "rank with sodomy", and accused the Apostles of being "a hotbed of unnatural vice". As a result Hobby took the decision to turn to a career in politics and to marry.

We don't know if Duncan ever bedded Swithinbank, about whom he wrote, he is "the most beautiful person I've ever met", and we don't know if he bedded Rupert Brooke [although it's probable], but Duncan did write to Lytton in 1908, "I'm not in love with him [Brooke], though it's occasionally occurred to me that I ought to be--but there are really too many drawbacks to him. His self-conceit is écrasant [crushing], and his general pose merely absurd." Then Lytton learned that Duncan was bedding Keynes, about which Holroyd writes: "Of all the amorous crises sprinkled through his life, this was perhaps the most wretched. It came as a complete shock.'' Lytton's brother James tried to lighten Lytton's pain by assuring him, ''There's hardly any affection'' between the two, at the same moment that Keynes wrote to Grant: ''Dear Duncan I love you too much and I can't now bear to live without you.'' Duncan Grant would be the love of both men's lives, their ''most intense sexual and emotional male love,'' writes Holroyd. With extreme generosity Lytton wrote to Keynes, ''I don't' hate you and if you were here now I should probably kiss you, except that Duncan would be jealous, which would never do!'' To which Keynes answered, ''Your letter made me cry.'' In reality, Lytton did hate Keynes as he'd never hated anyone in his life.

Both Lytton and Keynes were mere stations in Duncan's long and eventful journey through life, of dire importance to both, only momentary stopovers for handsome, sexually insatiable Duncan. It was Duncan who introduced Keynes into the Bloomsbury Set, from which Keynes would benefit, but the Bloomsbury Set would profit a thousandfold more, each person individually, and the Bloomsbury Set reputation incommensurably.

Following the death of Thoby, the house Vanessa, Virginia and Adrian Stephen bought began filling with visitors, a salon dedicated to conversation, where Clive Bell, Duncan Grant, Leonard Woolf and others would show up around ten at night and converse over whisky, cocoa and buns until two or three in the morning. Clive had pursued Vanessa for years now, and somehow Thoby's death led her to say yes to his insistent demands of marriage. She had hesitated and rightly so, as it was a mismatch. They would never divorce but Clive wandered in and out of the Bloomsbury Set until his death, and Duncan Grant would live with Vanessa at Charleston for 40 years, until she died, and then he. Lytton soon had a place on the couch and in the conversation with the others, that Virginia wrote were stodgy, all these serious young men pulling at their pipes and ''chuckling at some Latin joke'', wrote Holroyd, but she nonetheless found it infinitely superior to what she had known in Cambridge among other boys. ''Talking, talking, talking,'' wrote Virginia, perfectly summing up things, ''as if everything could be talked.'' But soon the masks dropped, apparently after Lytton began reciting his bawdy poems. Little by little he grew close to Virginia, admiring her intelligence, and truly fond of the first things she was writing, which, as a book reviewer, he knew how to evaluate. Clive Bell, now married and father of his and Vanessa's son Julian [named after Thoby], helped Virginia too in her writing, and slowly his lust displaced itself from Vanessa he now knew so well, to Virginia. Holroyd describes Virginia as a cock-teaser, which was the consequence of her abuse by her two stepbrothers, and soon she was providing not only access to Clive Bell, but inspired Lytton to the point that he asked her to marry him.

"As I did it, I saw it would be death if she accepted me, I managed, of course, to get out of it before the end of the conversation," stated Lytton in 1909, a quote thanks to Holroyd. Lytton wrote to Leonard Woolf, confiding that he was in a confused state of mind but that "I copulated with Duncan again this afternoon, and at the present he's in Cambridge copulating with Keynes". All of which was, and would be, the cornerstone of Bloomsbury Set sexuality. Woolf's response was to write Lytton, wondering if Virginia would have *him*, Woolf, for husband, as he had known and admired her for years. Despite Lytton and Woolf having had an affair in the past, Lytton wrote him that she would certainly accept his offer, "She really would. As it is, she is almost certainly in with me [Lytton], although she thinks she's not", and added, "Isn't it strange that I've never been in love with you? And I suppose I never shall." Lytton went on to say that he had offered marriage because of the "imagination of the paradise of married peace", but that now he would have to pull through on his own. Virginia wrote in her diary, twenty years later, that she had indeed loved Lytton, as their relationship was "an exquisite symphony of natures when all the violins get playing .... so deep, so fantastic", similar to what Bernard Swithinbank had written about Lytton, "When I left him I was in a condition. I didn't know one could have such affection without lust. But there it is. He's unique-- exquisite." Which brings only one conclusion: to know Lytton was to be drawn inextricably to him, something we have difficulty comprehending without having met him ourselves.

It was then that Lytton met George Mallory, manly shoulders, magnificent torso, wide smile, white teeth, blue eyes, a Praxiteles, whom Lytton said he spent hours a day admiring. Mallory had fallen head over heels for Lytton's brother James, who allowed Mallory to sleep with him once, but Mallory had copulated with Duncan, to use Lytton's term, although he apparently never gave Lytton a tumble.

As for Lytton's brother James, he comes through as someone solid, about whom an acquaintance wrote, "He seemed to have taken no pleasure or interest in material life or the physical world, and to exist only in the realms of pure intellect." He did offer Lytton good advice, and Lytton could always turn to him for support. James seemed to have been handsome enough to have made Mallory randy, but the love of James's life was Rupert Brooke, whom he convinced to take part in a camping expedition with others, Brooke's beauty unsettling the participants, boys and girls alike, and created an atmosphere of sexual tension, which Brooke worked off by daily hikes, ostensibly oblivious to the disruption he inspired, although certainly aware of James who followed him around like a lost puppy.

Rupert Brooke had been in love with Noel Oliver since she was 15, and now, aged 20, they were secretly engaged. There had never been sex between them, and indeed Brooke envisioned a marriage that would not be dirtied by something that would stain the purity of their love. Brooke was lustfully desired by everyone who came into contact with him, their love only second to his love for himself. He wrote Noel, ''I know how superb my body is, and how great my body strength,'' and ''I know that with my mind I could do anything. I know that I can be the greatest poet and writer in England,'' quotes from Holroyd of immense importance in our effort to understand this enigmatic lad.

Rupert Brooke is often cited for the letter he wrote concerning his plan to seduce a young friend. The letter is cold and calculating, and once he did get the lad's shorts down, one cares little for the lack of passion that followed. This was supposedly Brooke's first attempt at losing his burdensome virginity, homosexually speaking, as he had *apparently* ''known'' girls for some time. He was so startlingly good-looking that he was certainly prey from his earliest years, and because sex is what took place in boarding schools, days and especially nights, and given the nature of adolescent lust, the boy he said he'd seduced in his letter was most probably far from the first.

Rupert Brooke, 1887-1915

Whatever the case, Brooke maintained that at age 22 the time had come for sexual discovery, and that he'd chosen a boy, Denham Russell-Smith, rather than a girl because it would be easier. [A personal note. For a combination of reasons Rupert Brooke may well have had first sex at age 22. In my own case, raised a Mormon, the first time I ever touched a human being *in that way* was at age 26, *in the Louvre in Paris [!]*. In my autobiography, *Michael Hone: His World, His Loves*, I put the age at 22, simply because I felt that no one would believe I had gone so long without being with another, except, of course, fellow Mormons.]

Rupert Brooke

The problem evaluating Brooke's work is that one can't see the forest for the trees, the trees here being his beauty. He was president of the Cambridge Fabian Society and a founder of the Marlowe Society, a drama club in which he acted in its plays. How many students were members thanks to the club's literary appeal and how many were there--boys and girls--drawn by Brooke's beauty can't be known. Born in Rugby, in 1887, he is reputed for his First World War poetry, appeals for young men to engage in the services and commit mass suicide, his most celebrated poem being this:

If I should die, think only this of me:
That there's some corner of a foreign field
That is forever England. There shall be
In that rich earth a richer dust concealed;
A dust whom England bore, shaped, made aware,
Gave, once, her flowers to love, her ways to roam,
A body of England's, breathing English air,
Washed by the rivers, blest by suns of home.

Rupert Brook

Brooke apparently wanted to be heterosexual, but the problem was the fact ''that he still found it easier to have erections with men than with woman,'' wrote Holroyd, the conundrum of so many English boys who had discovered unhampered sex among themselves in prep schools (2), and never surmounted the sublimely erotic taste of first love with a boy: both male, both equally lustful, equally beautiful, both possessing the erect scepter that rules the world, and always will. Why they then turned to marriage may be explained, in some, by the coming of age: a slackening of the mind, of hope, of expectations, matched by a weakening of the body and a lessoning of virility.

Brooke had numerous lovers and friends, one of whom caught the ear of Winston Churchill who commissioned Brooke into the Royal Naval Volunteer Reserve, an honor Brooke accepted on the condition that his friend Denis Browne, a composer, be commissioned to. It was in Denis's arms on the island of Skyros that Brooke ... well, let Denis tell it: ''At 4 o'clock he became weaker, and at 4:46 he died, with the sun shining all round his cabin, and the cool sea-breeze blowing through the door and the shaded windows. No one could have wished for a quieter or a calmer end than in that lovely boy, shielded by the mountains and fragrant with sage and thyme.'' No one was luckier too to have a friend like Denis Browne.

Brooke died from a simple mosquito bite that had become infected. Denis died in battle at Gallipoli. His last letter was found in his wallet, that he'd put there knowing he hadn't long to live: ''I'm luckier than Rupert because I've fought. But there's no one to bury me as I buried him, so perhaps he's best off in the long run.''

Lytton had taken a cottage called The Lacket from 1912, where he worked on his book *Eminent Victorians*. It was there that his brother James introduced him to David [Bunny] Garnett and David's friend and part-time lover Frankie Birrell, whom Lytton took a shine to, both boys invited to The Lacket where David, just 22, wrote about Lytton: ''I was struck by his gentleness and his hospitality,'' Lytton now 35. Both David and Frankie had been Keynes's lovers, and of course David would soon become the love of Duncan Grant's life, Duncan who had lost George Mallory to marriage, who was at present mad for Adrian Stephen, he too soon to wed.

With the coming of war Lytton applied for exemption on the grounds of health and conscience. He appeared before an examining board in the company of a score of his supporters. Genuinely suffering from bad health since his birth, while waiting to be examined he sat on a cushion due to piles, not unnoticed by the board members. This and his hatred of war left no doubt that he would be found inapt for service.

In 1915 Lytton met the girl who would later shoot herself when she lost him, Dora Carrington, and although I don't like to give more than quotes from my sources, Holroyd's encapsulated portrait of her is too perfect not to reproduce in its entirety: ''Though Carrington had little glamour, she reached towards people out of her mystery; and they, responding to a strange allure, circled round, moved closer. Her manner was naturally flattering: she had a dazzling smile; and she made up to--almost flirted with--anyone she liked. She appeared extraordinarily alive at every point, consumed by the most vivid and confusing feelings about people, places, even objects.''

She has inspired several biographies, far more than Lytton Strachey has, that the reader can discover for himself/herself. Mark Gertler was one of the first to fall in love with her, both students at Slade School of Fine Arts. ''To touch her hand is bliss!'', Mark wrote, ''to kiss it Heaven itself! I have stroked her hair and I nearly fainted with joy.'' She was immediately attracted to Lytton, a man Gertler loathed [especially after Lytton had tried to bed him], perpetually asking himself how she could prefer a bugger--the name used for homosexuals then, a term used by homosexuals among themselves--to him. A student wrote that Gertler was ''popular with the girls and adored by them,'' as he was by many a boy too. Gertler wrote to Dora, ''I think you are the purest and *holiest* girl I have *ever* met ... I am going to devote my whole life to try and make you happy.'' Gertler was astoundingly handsome, and how he and Dora never really connected, like the proverbial two ships passing in the night, amounted to a crime, one that would see them both dead of self-inflicted gunshot wounds. Gertler asked her to marry him. She said no, adding, alas, that she nonetheless loved him. Unlike Virginia, Dora was no cock-tease, she was just Dora Carrington [of whom D.H. Lawrence wrote, ''in intimacy she was unscrupulous and dauntless as a devil incarnate,'' but then, he wrote lots of things, especially about homosexuals, that were groundless]. Gertler went through hell, as Holroyd brings us snippets of his writing to her: My passion ''is not lustful, but *beautiful*!'' ... you are wrong to ''think that I was vulgar and dirty'' ... I am ''not worthy of your company'' ... being ''*far* to vulgar and rough for you.'' One really does bleed for this boy, himself so talented, so *entire*, who will eventually put a bullet through his head.

Mark Gertler

As for Lytton, Virginia stated that now that he was in his late thirties he had become "curiously gentle, sweet tempered, considerate," assets Dora profited from, while he sunned in her adoration. They spent acres to time together, Lytton providing her with an education in literature, and it was he who took her virginity, a few months before she gave herself a second time, to Mark Gertler, so as not to lose him, Mark certainly believing he had been the first [telling her, afterwards, that if another man ever touched her he would kill himself].

So when Lytton visited his studio there were no clashes, and Lytton even bought one of Gertler's painting, the *Merry-Go-Round* for £10, found at the Tate and worth hundreds of thousands today.

The *Merry-Go-Round*, an example of Mark Gertler's art.

Lytton knew about what was going on between Dora and Mark, certainly wishing to be in Dora's shoes, but the situation itself only struck him as complicated, while it had life-and-death intensity for Gertler.

Finally Dora made a clean break. She told Mark she loved Lytton, and then she returned to him. Whereas Mark would have possessed her body with desire and fire, Lytton allowed her to kiss him lightly on the mouth, Lytton 37, Dora 24 and Mark 26. My heart breaks for Mark Gertler, who deserved so much more from the brief flame we call life.

With this infinitely sick triangle I'm going to bring the first half of Lytton's life to an end, his personal destiny disclosed in chapter one. Youth is the only period of a man's life worthy of great things, thanks to its hopes, promise, lust and infinite horizons. An example of which is Alexander, who left his mark at age 32, his lover, Hephaestion, dying a year earlier to prepare his entry into the Elysian Fields.

CHAPTER TEN

DUNCAN GRANT

PART I

The reason I do not write full biographies is that I'm spared having to relate the lives of this or that ancestor, nor even a subject's parents, unless they have special interest. I can skip through his education and come to the onset of puberty, the origin of the vital sap of life, and take it from there. I can also leave him at the onset of old age, when even the likes of Jean Cocteau, André Gide and Henry de Montherlant, the subjects of my recent *French Homosexuality* declared, when they were old, that they were freed from the need of searching for boys, especially Montherlant who up to then often spent 10 hours a day doing so. Now they were free. But free from what? Free from no longer sharing their bed with the warm, perishable heat of a young and lustful lover, his longing sighs in your ears? Not for me.

As the Bloomsbury Set was founded by Duncan Grant and, with his death at age 93 it came to an end, it is fitting that it is with Duncan that we bring this book to closure.

A self-portrait of Duncan Grant with turban, an evocation of the *Dreadnought* Hoax we discovered in the chapter on David Garnett.

Duncan Grant was a lesson in life in that he proved that one can go on a long, a very long time welcoming still another boy, one in need of the touch that will make him writhe, stretched out in your arms as your fingers, lips and tongue suspend time, offering a moment of shared passion that makes all of existence worth that one sacred instant.

Duncan Grant nude models.

Duncan was born in England but as a baby he was taken to India where, thanks to his father's rank in the army, he was surrounded by servants, servants that even bachelor soldiers could offer themselves, a sepoy to hand even a corporal his soap in the shower, another his towel, each careful not to infringe on the work of the other, as it was their only means of livelihood. The heat was debilitating, and only at the end of the afternoons did the soldiers leave their beds in preparation for the evening meal and drink that would plunge them into welcome oblivion. Military exercises were few and the favorite pastime was pig sticking. Relief could be found in the mountains, especially in Casmir (8).

At age 9 Duncan returned to England to begin his formal schooling. His mother's sister-in-law, Jane Strachey, Lady Strachey, had a hand in finding a school for him, Hillbrow, where she sent her own son James, two years younger than Duncan, a boy who would become one of Duncan's lovers, although James's older brother Lytton would have Duncan first. At Hillbrow Duncan was popular, largely due to his having lived in India and the tales of his sojourn there, and he was good at sports, always a way into the group that held the most power in prep schools. James Strachey was his best friend and he knew Rupert Brooke, also attending the school. The headmaster, Mr. Eden, liked to birch boys and fondle the younger ones in their baths, until a boy told his father and Eden was expulsed. Duncan recounted that Rupert went to the headmaster and helped him pack to leave, something Duncan was certain had saved Eden's life, as he had contemplated suicide until Rupert showed his compassion, Rupert only 15 at the time, already levelheaded--so much promise extinguished by his early death (2).

Douglas Blair Turnbaugh, in his excellent *Duncan Grant and the Bloomsbury Group*, 1987, relates a segment of Duncan's life that freed him from religious nonsense and got him thinking independently, all thanks to James Strachey. Duncan had been to a church service where he had the vision of Christ coming down the aisle and laying hands on him. He told James who suggested they look up Christianity in the *Encyclopedia Britannica*. We don't know which passage the boys read, but James asked, ''Do you mean to say you believe all this?'' Wrote Duncan later: ''My Christianity fell away from me like a mantle.'' Nietzsche too had removed the shackles of superstition very young. Nietzsche wrote, ''God, the immortality of the soul, redemption, the 'beyond' were concepts I had no time to pay attention to--not even as a child, perhaps because I wasn't childish enough. I was too curious, too questioning, too exuberant to put up with a concept as crude as the existence of a god. For me, God was an invitation *to not think*.''

Duncan stayed with the Stracheys until his parents returned from Rangoon. It was at Hillbrow prep school that his talent for art was first recognized and encouraged, followed, at age 14, by St. Paul's day school. He took military training but was found inept, always dropping his rifle, and in his studies he was branded an imbecile, especially due to his complete ignorance in mathematics [which didn't stop him from having his affair with the mathematical genius, Keynes, and become the love of Keynes's life]. In fact, he was found only suited for art, notably after he won prizes that St. Paul's offered in painting. At age 17 he went to the Westminster School of Art, taking up residence with the Stracheys in a seven-storey home Duncan's mother Ethel called a palace. She and Duncan's father Bartle were housed there too on occasion, in a hugely numerous family, a building that was vast, albeit with only one bathroom.

A revealing incident took place when he was 17. He had been sent to the South of France where, on the way, in Paris, he bought a book *How We Lost Our Virginity*, exactly what a young lad would buy and of course use to stimulate masturbation, although not that much outward stimulation was necessary in pre-pornography years when a bare shoulder, or an ankle or bicep [depending on one's sexual bent] could spurn crazed episodes of self-abuse, as it was called at the time. The period was also known for the Masturbation Panic, that I would like to take a moment to explain: The cause of homosexuality was often attributed to masturbation, but from the 1700s to the 1900s there was even a masturbation panic, caused by the beliefs of certain doctors, most notably a doctor whose name has come down to us, Simon-André Tissot, who claimed that the loss of an ounce of semen equaled the loss of forty ounces of blood, a crippling factor that could lead to the loss of eyesight, to diseases and, due to increased blood flow to the brain, insanity, consequences far more severe than religious repercussions due to the nefarious, unnatural act of self-pleasuring, the mortal enemy of procreation. In the mid-1850s it was blamed for the corruption of morals, as well as vile thoughts that threatened the salvation of the soul itself, accompanied by the exhaustion of the entire nervous system. Boys were ordered to do physical exercises until they dropped from fatigue, to take cold showers, and fathers were advised to tie up their hands at night [presumably behind their backs, although the most exquisite sensation could then be enjoyed by gently rubbing oneself against one's mattress, as the reader well knows]. Some surgeons recommended replacing the testicles of masturbators with healthy ones [which could lead to castration because the new testicles were rejected by the body, and death if the surgery was done in unclean surroundings, often the case in those times].

Intercourse too was to be restricted to procreation, because if it were practiced too often the result would be the same as for masturbation, the proof being the loss of energy and extreme fatigue after spilling one's seed. This was reinforced by the fact that men in asylums openly and often masturbated. The final choice was between going to Hell or ending up insane, little wonder the period was known for its masturbation panic. Today things have changed, thanks to Internet, to the extent that a lad is considered a prude if he refrains from jerking off in the presence of a college roommate, as well as lots of other damning things open to the brave at heart.

Lytton Strachey was five years older than Duncan, a student of Trinity College, Cambridge. Cambridge had freed his mind intellectually and unbridled his sexuality. Lady Strachey had spent a great deal of her life in India, her father in the government and her future husband, Richard, one of his secretaries, both serving during the horrific Mutiny of 1857 (8). Lady Strachey had lost an eye, and had trained herself in Braille as she knew she was losing sight in the other, something that tells us a great deal about the force of nature found in all the Stracheys. She was a feminist, and intellectually suited to accept her sons' homosexuality. Clive Bell whom we met in the first chapter was already part of the Strachey entourage, as was Roger Fry, both meeting Duncan for the first time, both his future lovers.

Duncan went to day schools and so may have escaped early carnal knowledge. He later recalled his first sexual experience to the love of the last half of his life, Paul Roche, omitting, alas, his age at the time. He was in the National Gallery looking at a painting when an older boy came up behind him, reached around and gently rubbed his penis through his trousers. ''We were alone in the room--he pulled out my cock and very soon I came onto the floor. I rubbed the mess with my foot.'' The boy was a Swede that Duncan greatly liked and rendezvoused with several times. When the Swede left, Duncan wondered if he could produce the same sensation on his own. He did to himself what the Swede had done and came, his first experience with masturbation. [Men rarely tell the truth about their initial sexual experience, and it would be surprising if Duncan hadn't already known what was going on thanks to his prep-school chums.] Whatever the case, from then on the floodgates were open.

Duncan's book on how to lose one's virginity was discovered and the boy was sent to a series of doctors because the adults were certain he was on the edge of dementia, until finally he had the good fortune of finding a doctor who told him he had nothing to worry about, that, in other words, his playing with himself was of no consequence. The story is important because even without the doctor's council, Duncan was a boy who had, from an extremely early age, accepted himself, accepted his sexuality and shucked religious voodooism. Meaning that he was in no way an imbecile. In 1906, at age 21, he went to Italy with his mother, where he discovered marvelous Siena, Rome and copied paintings in the Uffizi in Florence.

Lytton Strachey was greatly drawn to new ideas, the reason he followed English philosopher G.E. Moore so closely, Moore who gave the Bloomsbury Set a core of rationalism, ''a desire to employ the tools of reason in order to arrive at a more lucid view of the world,'' writes Francis Spalding in her excellent *Duncan Grant*, 1997, and, Moore went on, there was nothing of greater value in life than ''the pleasure of human intercourse and the enjoyment of beautiful objects'', all of huge appeal to Lytton, Lytton who knew the secrets of the love lives of the members of the Apostles, covered in the second chapter, and the sexual happenings at Cambridge, which he detailed to Duncan, eager for such knowledge. Lytton, who didn't hesitate to kiss Roger Fry on the mouth in a busy London street, knew that the best way with a boy was to firmly grasp his crotch. The boy would either buck and run off or, more likely, get hard and give in. Such is what happened early on with Duncan. Lytton immediately wrote to Maynard Keynes: ''It's happened ... so violent, and how supreme are the things of this earth! I've managed to catch a glimpse of Heaven. It's Duncan!'' And later, ''I want him to love me as I love him, and to deserve his love. All that's obvious and before my nose is that he's absolutely mine. I haven't the nerve to think of the future.'' Duncan returned to Paris where he was joined by Edgar Duckworth, called Dicker, Lytton's former lover that Lytton had lost to Keynes. Duncan loyally wrote to Lytton saying he ''had fallen in love with him and he with me,'' [the exact words Duncan had used in his love affair with Hobby], a quote from Turnbaugh. Duncan also lost his heterosexual cherry as it was the tradition of the times for a father or an uncle to give a lad money so he could have first sex with a prostitute. In Duncan's case an uncle came through, in Paris, with 18 francs, Duncan aged 21.

At the time Keynes was with Arthur Hobhouse, Hobby, whom Lytton had loved before him. When Hobhouse at first avoided Keynes, Lytton, who knew him well, wrote that Keynes should simple ''rape'' him. Whatever took place, they did end up in the same bed. [Hobby was so cautious of showing himself during sex that his lover Dillwyn Knox wrote to W.H. Auden, ''You will hardly believe it but I don't know whether Hobby is circumcised or not--you can't conceive his precautions.'' Hobby's sexuality, along with that of Rupert Brooke, were the most enigmatic of them all.] Keynes wanted Duncan too, and wrote Lytton: ''I am in love with your being in love with another'' and offered Lytton a piece of advice, ''don't go buggering him, it would be too damned easy'' [whatever that meant]. Things nonetheless cooled, and Strachey wrote Keynes, ''Our relation has settled down into--an affectionate indifference, punctuated with weekends of lust,'' which, in a nutshell, summarizes the impermanence of homosexual love.

Maynard Keynes.
Alas, there are simply no photos of Lytton and Keynes in their youth, nor of Hobhouse, other than this one of Maynard.

Duncan returned to London for a short stay, going to the Apostles where he could literally choose a boy like one would in a whorehouse. His choice was Arthur Hobhouse, whom Duncan said ''was a Greek god''. Together they went to Florence and Siena. Back in London, at Hobhouse's manor, they had been vocal in their lovemaking, alerting the butler who told Arthur's mother. Duncan was ordered out of the house and returned to La Palette and Paris where found time for a new boy, a short-term affair with Maxwell Armfeld [who ended up marrying, like most men then].

Things became more complicated when Lytton's brother James Strachey admitted to Duncan that he loved him too, which led to Duncan's doing both brothers at the same time, a kind of birthday present as it was 1906 and Duncan had just turned 21. He left for Paris where he studied painting at the Académie Julian. He did a lot of copying in the Louvre, as a painter has the right to do, even today, on acceptance of his dossier. We don't know how much sex took place because there was no Strachey-like witness to write to an eager Keynes, but, as said, we do know he lost his heterosexual cherry.

Lytton Strachey, Dora Carrington and James Strachey [*and* another poor-quality photo].

In Paris Duncan received the visit of Hobby with whom he fell in love. He felt it honorable to inform Lytton who told Hobhouse's lover Keynes. At the time Duncan was 21, Lytton 26, James 19, Keynes 23 and Hobby 20. Only later photos of Hobhouse exist, but in his youth he was described as an irresistible beauty. Duncan wrote Lytton: ''He [Hobhouse] told me he loved me as much as is possible for him to love anybody. It makes no difference between you and me.'' Lytton did not agree: ''We can like each other as before, and kiss each other, but we can never be alone together.'' When Duncan read the letter he broke into tears and had to take to his bed, ill with depression. Lytton was self-aware enough to realize that it was useless to beg Duncan for unwilling kisses, even if he knew that Duncan would eventually return to him, perhaps for no other reason than Duncan's need for constant sex, and he knew from what Keynes had told him that Hobby didn't desire or need much physical contact--leaving Duncan with an unattended erection. Hobhouse presumably sublimated his wants in religion, his need for God greater than his need for intimacy, after which he devoted himself to politics and marriage.

In Paris Duncan continued his painting classes, his copying in the Louvre of the Masters, joyfully sketching nudes at the Académie and passing time in cafés over coffee with new acquaintances. He attended the Quatr'z'Arts, a ball organized by the Beaux-Arts, a once-a-year student rite of Spring, about which Duncan wrote to Lytton: ''I have seen Lust walking about undisguised, debauchery carried to its limits, drunkenness and frenzy, everywhere prevalent.'' The year that Duncan saw it the subject of the ball was Cleopatra, her breasts displayed and her servants nude (1).

He returned to London where Lytton introduced him to the Stephen family, Vanessa Stephen with whom he would sire a child, Virginia Stephen, soon Virginia Woolf, and Adrian Stephen, another future lover. Clive Bell was present, whom Vanessa later married. The Bloomsbury Set came into being, the Stephens, Duncan and the Stracheys founding members. Hobhouse was on the periphery, whom Duncan continued to long for.

Amusingly, Duncan met other groups of people who were frankly too heterosexually oriented to be of interest to him, but proof that despite my insistence on recounting his male-male adventures, male-female intercourse flourished too [from which the ever-increasing French population benefits].

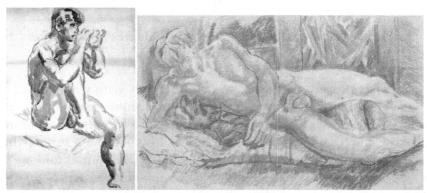

Nudes by Duncan Grant.

Maynard Keynes was offered a lectureship in economics at Cambridge where Duncan occasionally visited him, aware that Keynes knew about every sexual adventure in Duncan's life, thanks to Lytton's letters to Keynes. Keynes is a huge mystery. Not good-looking, he nonetheless attracted boys, supposedly due to a mixture of charm, frankness that increased a person's self-knowledge, but whose common sense, said Lytton, ''was enough to freeze a volcano''. Lytton continues: ''Keynes sits like a decayed and amorous spider at King's [College Cambridge], weaving purely imaginary webs, noticing everything that happens and doesn't happen,'' a quote brought to us by Frances Spalding. Clive Bell found him too cocky due to his educated, wealthy parents and Keynes's being brought up in Cambridge among what Britain had best in intelligentsia. But far more likely, Keynes was polite, affectionate, never arrogant, endearing, a man people were simply happy to be around.

Duncan now fell in love with him, and later told Paul Roche, the most intimate friend he would ever have, that he had never been closer to any human being as he had been to Maynard Keynes. Keynes offered Duncan self-awareness and freed Duncan's mind to face any intellectual challenge, as well as to fully accept his homosexuality. During one short separation from Keynes, Duncan wrote in a letter: "Dearest, at this moment I would give my soul to the Devil if I could kiss you and be kissed."

They did get together and toured the Orkney Islands, a period that Lytton referred to as their honeymoon. Lytton was bitter at having lost Duncan, but bitter too because he had written to both Keynes and Duncan, before he knew of their liaison, letters both boys shared, those to Keynes describing Duncan as wonderful, those to Duncan stating that Keynes lacked virility.

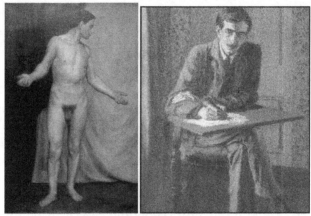

Keynes by Duncan.

In Cambridge Keynes was enjoying his leadership in the Apostles, debauching the new embryos, discovering that homosexuality was "absolutely universal" there, and although Duncan was ever randy, he apparently could not fill all of Keynes's sexual demands. Keynes continued teaching, writing this about a women's class he gave: "I seem to hate every movement of their minds. The minds of men even when they themselves are stupid and ugly, never appear to me so repellent."

Then Duncan, now 24, wrote to James Strachey: "I no longer feel myself to be in love with a person [Keynes] who sometimes bores me and sometimes irritates me, and from whom I can live apart without being unhappy, however much I may like to be with him." [In homosexual couplings the boys then simply separate; it's far more complicated when married.] Duncan continued his painting, taking on new models who would sexually service him, as modeling was often a way for hustlers to earn money, posing in the nude and its consequences on the artist, as when Duncan was turned on by a boy's cock hardening before his eyes, the come-hither invitation in his eyes, in exchange for a few coins.

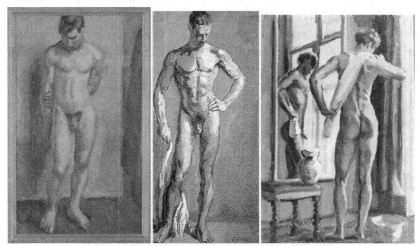

Nudes posing for Duncan.

In London Duncan continued his courses in painting at Slade School of Art, but it was with the Bloomsbury Set that things became dynamic, and the members established firm ground rules: the obligation to be freethinking and unhampered in all things; to pursue literature, art, and philosophy; and to have limitless sex and form solid friendships [all of which they lived up to throughout their entire lives]. It was then that Duncan took part in the *Dreadnought* Hoax described in the chapter on David Garnett. He entered into triangular sex with fellow members, with friends of members and with the friends of friends of the members, the Apostles, short-lived associations like the Friday Club, and boys he met during the exhibitions Duncan frequented and would soon give. Presumably Keynes was providing him with embryos, boys who would allow Keynes to have his way with them in exchange for introductions to the supremely handsome Rupert Brooke and Duncan Grant. He began to expose his art in galleries where he earned modest sums. He fell in love with Adrian Stephen, whom he had known for some time and rediscovered during the *Dreadnought* Hoax, Adrian 27.

Lacking funds of his own, Duncan gratefully accepted Keynes's invitation to explore Greece where the love of male nudes was limitlessly on display in sculptures, which inspired him to pose naked for Keynesian photos, photos he allowed Keynes to later show around. Homoeroticism was the link that bound the two friends, as Keynes would continue to introduce Duncan to boys who had homosexual leanings, a benefit to the boys too, especially as Duncan had returned from Greece relaxed, never looking more handsome, his body integrally bronzed. Sex between Keynes and him continued, something Duncan had especially appreciated in Greece where he was continually in rut and, stretched out over a bed in the stifling heat, would allow himself to be attended to by Keynes who asked for nothing reciprocal in return. Duncan was now 25.

Back in London Duncan sold his paintings mostly to friends, one of whom was Vanessa Bell. Roger Fry entered the picture with his 1910 Post-Impressionists exhibition, eventually of such import [despite all the criticism, as seen in Fry's chapter] that the Bloomsbury Set, known mostly for its literature, gained a growing reputation in painting, one of huge consequence when Duncan's work finally took off.

Vanessa by Duncan. They traveled extensively together, their favorite stopovers: Paris and St. Tropez.

Problems were now brewing between Vanessa and her husband Clive who took sexual liberties with Vanessa's sister Virginia, as well as reunite with the woman who had presumably taken his cherry when very young, and had taught him a thing or two. Duncan went off on another trip with Keynes, this to Sicily, with a stopover so he could spend some quality times with Adrian in Capri, deserting Keynes who had nonetheless been forewarned by Duncan. Such would be Keynes's destiny, perhaps one of the reasons he later settled into a twenty-year-long marriage with a ballerina. But Duncan was a beauty, the world his oyster, and men like Keynes were there to fill in the gaps between his love interests [and also help him out, as Keynes was doing now, by offering him gifts like the trip to Sicily].

In London Duncan discovered Diaghilev's Ballets Russes, and Nijinsky, and like generations before and after him, Duncan was smitten to the core. Adrian in the meantime grew cooler, due perhaps to the interference of the segment of him that needed heterosexual contacts.

Then Destiny came through with the offer of a mural that would decorate the Borough Polytechnic:

The Bathers

Men bathing naked is the ultimate transfiguration of homoerotic desire. Duncan himself wrote that he "longed to get out and live the rest of my life among the beautiful youths I saw playing in and out of the mirror-like sea."

That dream took on a certain reality in his 1911 mural at the London Borough Polytechnic, that the *National Review* warned would "deteriorate young and sensitive minds", leading to "degeneracy", the desire for homoerotic coupling beyond the comprehension of the working-class students of the Polytechnic. The Review was correct in the sense that the mural gave Duncan a chance to express his love of naked bathers, and as early as 1907 he had written to Lytton Strachey from Florence where he watched the "miraculously lovely" young men bath naked in the Arno. Duncan knew about and had certainly participated in the nude bathing that took place around the Serpentine in London, where the working classes met for leisure and physical recreation, and the nearby bushes for exchanges of rapid mutual orgasms [at times a free exchange, at times gay-for-pay].

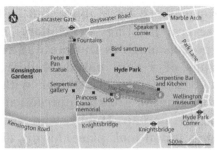

The Serpentine

Many talented people never find fame because they lack the right contacts and luck. Duncan had both, in this case it was his lover Roger Fry who got him the Polytechnic commission, Fry's idea being to create an athletic modernistic mural showing recreation all Londoners had access to. The result was a huge painting of almost life-size swimmers that homosexuals see as a declaration of same-sex desire, in harmony with nature, the basis of Bloomsbury eroticism.

The commission of *The Bathers* was followed by other good news, the return of Adrian to Duncan's bed. Duncan was also "with" James Strachey again, Lytton's younger brother, but this was short lived, certainly due to the lack of beauty in both brothers, something their intellectual brilliance could not compensate for.

Other *Bathers* by Duncan.

Duncan met George Mallory thanks to the good offices of the Stracheys, this time James who made the introductions, James who had been repeatedly propositioned by Mallory and had given in one time. In 1913 Duncan did several paintings of Mallory, in the nude, for which Mallory wanted to pose as much as Duncan wanted him to do so. Duncan also took photographs of a very naked Mallory, as seen in Mallory's chapter. Duncan had a memorable dinner with Mallory and Rupert Brooke, Brooke whom Duncan greatly appreciated but at the time Brooke was obsessed with a boy, perhaps Hobby, who was homosexually virginal. So apparently nothing sexual took place, hardly of importance to Brooke who was used to being relentlessly sought after by both sexes. The reason that Mallory and Duncan didn't hook up for a longer period may have been Duncan's continued efforts to regain Adrian Stephen's love, and Mallory's dance card was otherwise filled too. Duncan had another insistent follower, Gordon Luce, who wrote to Keynes in the hope of his using his influence to arrange a meeting with Duncan, Luce who ended one of his letters to Keynes: "Love to D--if only he needed it!", a quote brought to us by Francis Spalding. Luce was an Apostle who, during a trip to Burma, fell in love with a Burmese girl that he wished to marry but was frustrated by his family and friends who vehemently advised him against it. The marriage eventually took place and Luce became a father. Of his wife he said that his only wish was "that she were a boy". It was at this time, too, that Fry put on his second, and far more successful, exhibition of Post-Impressionists, and introduced Picasso to Duncan. The ever-faithful Fry pushed Duncan's works, telling one and all he had genius. Duncan's paintings were included in the Fry exhibition and some were sold.

Mallory by Duncan.

Vanessa became attached to Fry and it was now that Fry opened the Omega Workshops, detailed in his chapter, that were also showrooms for perspective buyers. Duncan participated, designing things like boxes and fans, on one of which he had two figures kissing, the sales adding greatly to his income. Vanessa was there and bit-by-bit her fondness for Roger was replaced by love for Duncan. He accepted Vanessa's invitation to her Wissett farmhouse where they bathed and slept together. Duncan was now 28 and soon to be the father of Vanessa's child Angelica.

He continued to see and bed Vanessa's brother Adrian, which apparently she and Adrian's other sister Virginia found amusing, although not Duncan who had been fond of the boy for years and did not have near-enough access to him. Adrian continued to see girls and attempted to find something to do with his life, having tried his hand at acting, at becoming a doctor and a barrister, failing in all. Adrian was described as charm personified, although apparently lacking in good looks, which in no way hindered Duncan's affection for him. Adrian and Duncan would remain loyal to each other to the last days of their lives, Adrian dying in 1948, his wife committing suicide immediately afterwards.

Two of Duncan's paintings of Adrian.

One of Adrian's friends was Francis Birrell, Frankie, who would soon introduce Duncan to the love of the first half of Duncan's life, David Garnett, age 22 then, seven years younger than Duncan. I've covered David's life in his chapter, but I didn't tell all.

Before their affair enflamed the lives of both, they repeatedly met at various parties sponsored by the usual men, a party organized by Adrian Stephan, another by Keynes, and one by the Stracheys. Duncan invited him to pose, certainly nude, and soon they were sleeping together in Duncan's studio, which Clive Bell knew about and wrote, ''it was all very promiscuous'' [promiscuous because Bell knew Duncan was bedding every boy in reach, and he probably knew about his liaison with his own wife Vanessa and, of course, Bell himself had slept with Duncan]. It was also at this time that D.H. Lawrence came out with his terrible tirade against the Bloomsbury Set in general, against David's homosexuality and his homosexual friends in particular. Lawrence added this to the damning letter he wrote to David, quoted in Garnett's chapter: ''You can come away and grow whole, and love a woman and marry her, and make life good, and be happy. Now David, in the name of everything that is called love, leave this set [Bloomsbury] and stop this blasphemy against love.'' Very strange views, to my mind, from such an admirable writer and man-of-the-world. Quentin Bell, Vanessa's son, who later became a writer and art historian, was the first to write that Lawrence's reaction was in reality his fear of his own homosexual tendencies.

While this homosexual activity was going on, Vanessa Bell complained that she was still waiting for the fruit of her intercourse with Duncan, writing, ''No little Grant has yet had a chance to come into existence,'' apparently not for lack of Grant's trying. As mentioned before, Vanessa was no tyro to sex, fully participating in what she herself called fucking and sucking, in large part due to her stepbrothers.

A Grant painting of heterosexual felicity.

Elsewhere things were hunky-dory. Keynes was working himself up through the ranks of government, earning a reputation that is sterling to this very day. Lytton was writing and relentlessly pursued by Dora Carrington. Duncan was drawing, Garnett was continuing his education, Vanessa was awaiting her happy event [the child who would deeply disappoint her by marrying the boy, David Garnett, that Duncan was currently screwing], Vanessa's little boy Julian was discovering his love for dancing in public, totally naked [that Dora Carrington found wonderful, and wished she too could be so uninhibited], and Vanessa's husband Clive was off somewhere with his mistress Mary Hutchinson. Only Roger Fry, deeply in love with Vanessa, was left out in the cold.

In 1915 David Garnett went off to France to do some volunteer work there with Quakers, leaving Duncan depressed at his absence. The war was underway, during which Duncan sold no paintings. Only the slight income from the Omega Workshops [and probably handouts from friends who truly loved him, like Keynes whose government work left him financially flush]. When David returned from France he and Duncan took up farming to avoid the draft. Duncan's father visited and met David whom he called Mr. Garbage, probably not to his face. Vanessa came by too and left her two small sons, Quentin and Julian for the summer. As usual Keynes came through by guaranteeing payment of the rent for the farm, and in addition he bought several of Duncan's paintings, although Duncan's work was extremely limited due to farm chores. David found out he too could count on Keynes, whom he went to when things were not right with Duncan, and that Keynes, who thoroughly knew and loved Duncan, would give him most valued advice. In all domains, in all portions of Keynes's life, he came through as a wonderful, humane human being, and his propensity to confide in his diary, his tell-all about the boys he'd had, their beauty, dick size and what they did together [with a tendency for wanking, to use the English term], make him more human still.

David by Duncan. David said of Grant, "He is the most entertaining companion I have ever known."

Despite living with David, Duncan was still bedding Vanessa, and wrote in his diary, "I copulated on Saturday with Vanessa with great satisfaction to myself physically." He went on to write that women were "convenient" in that there was no "spunk" to clean up. He also complained of David's not particularly liking to be "buggered", although Duncan admitted: "not that my god I don't enjoy the excitement of it myself." Adrian also observed to a friend that Duncan "is rather like a woman in certain of his tendencies," clearly indicating that he liked being taken. Because Duncan was "seeing" others at the same time, one of whom was apparently, again, James Strachey, he wrote in his diary: "Perhaps I am too wicked to be happy or to make anyone else happy."

Despite Duncan's doubts about himself, there's no doubt he was in the midst of life. In the midst of living. Using and being used, the unique reason for our existence.

Vanessa was finally pregnant and Keynes, ever to the rescue, bought her a landau for the child and a horse so she could move about. He saw to Duncan too, by getting him the best seats to a Diaghilev ballet, alas without Nijinsky as the two men had had a parting of the ways [the lives of both can be found in my book *Venice*].

The birth of Vanessa's baby would be politely attributed to her husband Clive Bell, and it was Duncan himself who sent him a telegram where he was hold up with Mary Hutchinson, informing him about the girl's arrival, without a hint that it was he, Duncan, responsible. David Garnett saw the baby and immediately decided they would marry. That he finished by doing so--and that Angelica would later fall in love with him--is one of life's truly astonishing quirks.

Christmas 1918 was a moment of growing separation between David and Duncan. ''Duncan's feelings for me have altered very considerably since Christmas. It is not that he is not fond of me but that he feels that I am in some way a weight--a drag, a bore, and that he feels his path is not mine.'' As mentioned in his chapter, David liked girls and had never ceased shacking up with one, which didn't stop him from being furious when he came upon Duncan in bed with Edward Wolfe, infuriating Duncan too, who accused David of showing up without warning, the Bloomsbury Set at its finest, homosexuality at its purest, as faithfulness does not exist in Sodom, and it never will [and, anyway, faithfulness wasn't part of the Bloomsbury Set charter]. For all the ups and downs both went through, David Garnett was a fine man and Duncan had been lucky to have him; in fact, they both had been lucky during the time they shared.

Roger Fry distanced himself from the Bloomsbury Set, his contribution infinitely greater than anything the Set had to offer him, especially in affection, although he would *always* be in the wings to help when he could.

Clive Bell established himself in Paris where he was welcomed by Jean Cocteau, Satie, Picasso, André Gide and others, luminaries that made up a period on which I've written extensively in my book *The Belle Epoque*. He, Fry and Garnett will now *partially* leave the stage, replaced by others for whom the Bloomsbury Set was still a tempting light.

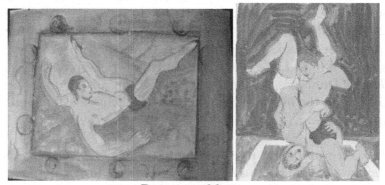

Duncan athletes

PART II

Part II will be shorter than Part I because the vital, exciting time in a man's life is his youth, replaced later by the memories of his youth. There will also be no closing picture of Duncan Grant. In their statues the Greeks portrayed a man, no matter when he died, around age 16, when his beauty was such that the poets reserved him for the love of the gods. I believe in that tradition and will therefore not show the revenges of time, that raise men to the height of physical exquisiteness, only to plunge them into the depths of disgraceful, degrading decay. Why do we fear death, I often wonder, when it is only eternal sleep, and not old age, the true human night?

A landmark event in Duncan's life was his exhibition at the Paterson-Carfax Gallery in 1920, Duncan now 35. Faithful Roger Fry was there and wrote in the *New Statesman* that Duncan's work was full of "transparent sincerity and simplicity" [although some Bloomsbury Set members thought he could have been a smidgen more admiring] and Clive Bell wrote in several of his publications that Duncan Grant is, "in my opinion, the best English painter alive" [much better]. Lytton Strachey bought *Juggler and Tightrope Walker*, paying a whopping £60, which he could afford thanks to the success of his book *Eminent Victorians*. Fry, Bell and Strachey, three former lovers whose love had not be tarnished by the march of time.

This exhibition was followed by another with 21 watercolors. The money earned was placed with Keynes who multiplied it like the biblical loaves of bread, which allowed Duncan to vacation in Rome with Vanessa, apparently chastely, both joined by Keynes. Duncan went on alone to Paris where he lunched with André Gide and his extremely young lover--later film director--Marc Allégret (1). Marc was not at all hostile to relations with older men, having slept with Cocteau, and Duncan later told Vanessa that he had been drawn to the boy, without offering details.

Back in England life was routine. Duncan painted while Vanessa cared for him and her sons Julian and Quentin, both occupied in collecting moths [Julian would soon be off to Cambridge and the bed of Russian spy Anthony Blunt, and Quentin would leave school at 17, travel and take up writing and painting, both successfully]. David Garnett soon married, as did the supremely homosexual George Mallory. Even Keynes would take a wife, Lydia Lopokova. Duncan wouldn't marry, but he did live with Vanessa for forty years, until her death. In the meantime Duncan's paintings were selling enough so he could finally care for Vanessa, Angelica and Vanessa's boys.

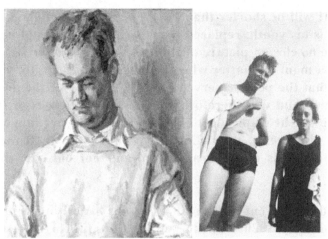

Quentin and Julian Bell with his mother Vanessa, Vanessa who was called Nessa by family and friends.

Duncan did continue to have adventures, something Vanessa knew she could do nothing about. He became attracted to two students, Douglas Davidson first, and then his younger brother Angus, to the apparent amusement of Quentin, old enough to know what was going on.

Angus Davidson by Duncan Grant.

Through the Davidson brothers Duncan met the sculptor Stephen Tomlin, known as Tommy, the high point of Duncan's love life in 1923, a boy for whom he sat for a bust portrait. Tommy, bisexual, had much earlier been the love interest of both Davidson brothers.

Duncan's bust by Tommy Tomlin. Tommy would soon marry Lytton Strachey's niece Julia Strachey, around the same time Keynes and Garnett and Mallory also took wives.

Vanessa was always present, traveling widely with Duncan, to France, Spain and Italy, always by his side, lightheartedly friendly to his lovers, lovers in the plural, as no one person had yet filled the place of David Garnett in Duncan's affections.

In 1924 Duncan left for Berlin to visit a boy eight years younger than he, Duncan now 39, a boy Duncan had met in London when he was passing through a year earlier, Franzi von Haas. Franzi toured the city with Duncan, the most sexually liberated in the world at the time, that the English visited in droves for sex with healthy, muscular lads that cost nearly nothing because soldiers, sailors and school boys knew they could earn pocket change just by allowing themselves to be blown, this not counting professional hustlers in the thousands (10). We don't know the details of what went on, but when Duncan returned to London he entered into a relationship with Edward Sackville-West, the brother of Vita who, the reader may remember, was Virginia Woolf's lover, and had also been the lover of Roy Campbell's wife, which forced Campbell, a member of the Bloomsbury Set, to flee to Toledo Spain.

Edward Sackville-West

Edward was sixteen years younger than Duncan, was said to have been effeminate, a boy who preferred the company of women, often proposing marriage, but was drawn, sexually, to hirsute men of brawn from the army and the working classes. Eddy had been going with Tommy Tomlin but was soon bedded by Duncan who apparently fell in love with him. Unlike David Garnett, Duncan wouldn't have to force Eddy to take the role played by women. Duncan wrote to David telling him of his new find and then went off to Venice for a vacation with Vanessa. It was perhaps because Duncan needed a physical exchange more reciprocal than what he had with Eddy that Eddy was replaced by a handsome, virile painter, Peter Morris, so hugely attractive that Vanessa was afraid of losing Duncan to him. Duncan had hidden his affair with the effeminate Edward from public view, but loved showing off Peter.

Peter Morris by Duncan.

In 1927 Duncan wintered in Cassis in the South of France with Vanessa and Angelica, where the English swarmed to escape the cold and wet British climate, a place where, in those times, no one would think of going during the summer due to the heat and implacable sun. The villa they took was stormed by friends from London, as well as new friends, mostly English, who lived in the vicinity. Peter Morris was off traveling through the Sahara so Duncan felt free to bed whomever he wished, one affair even with a woman, actress Valerie Taylor.

Their Villa Corsica was in utter chaos due to the continuous stream of visitors, Quentin escaping the mayhem by residing in Paris where his father Clive Bell lived and refused to meet his son because, he felt, either people would know of the parenthood between them and discover how old Clive was, or the girls Clive sought would take Quentin for Clive's lover, and flee him. As for Julian Bell, he was a highly popular student at Cambridge where he made feminine conquests and where he became the lover, as said, of the Cambridge Russian spy Anthony Blunt, his teacher, while fighting off Guy Burgess who ached to get into his pants. Julian told his mother about his affair with Blunt; she wrote back to say how happy she was at his sharing his activities with her. When David Garnett heard about Julian humping Blunt, he went to Cambridge where it was rumored he had Julian too, after sleeping for years with his father Duncan, after years of watching Julian grow to manhood, Garnett who would soon marry Julian's half-sister Angelica. Again, it may have been pure Bloomsbury, but it was nonetheless mindboggling if true that Garnett really did sleep with Julian.

David Garnett by Dora Carrington and David Garnett by Vanessa.

Duncan met George Bergen through mutual friends. George had won a scholarship to Yale School of Art, no mean feat, and at age 18 he won a Prix de Rome. Of Russian origin, Bergen made it to England thanks to his acquaintance with male friends, friends he played off against each other as he rose through the heights of the British aristocracy. He received a commission to paint the walls of Gerald Chichester's manor house, a joint commission with Duncan, which led to their sleeping together, and loyalty between the two that would last until their deaths, despite Bergen becoming the lover of Duncan's daughter Angelica, years later when she visited New

York where Bergen was living. Duncan offered Bergen an exhibition in his own studio, followed by another in 1932 at the Lefevre Gallery, for which David Garnett wrote the introduction to the exhibition catalogue. Bergen went to Hollywood to paint the stars, notably Charles Chaplin. He later settled and died in New York. Duncan had been deeply in love with him, their liaison lasting 18 months.

George Bergen

In 1931 Duncan had an exhibition at the Cooling Galleries of 51 of his paintings, among them one of Jimmy Seean, an American Duncan met through mutual friends, a foreign correspondent who spoke several languages fluently, had been married and divorced two times, and had been Eddy Sackville-West's lover for two years, Eddy who wrote to Duncan telling him that he had destroyed his life by taking Jimmy from him, and vowed that he would never forgive nor speak to Duncan again. Duncan was still with Bergen at the time, but as Bergen was away in the South of France, he took up with Jimmy. Frances Spalding offers us an amusing story of Jimmy coming across a guy in a bar. They got to talking and after several cocktails each admitted to the other that he had carnally known Duncan, Jimmy at the present time and the man 25 years earlier, who stated that he had not only loved Duncan, but that Duncan had been his first love, the boy who took his virginity.

Off for work in Rome, Jimmy invited Duncan to drop by which Duncan did, in the belief that he would be spending a great deal of time with Jimmy. To his surprise this was not the case, and one day Duncan arrived at the apartment they shared to find a note from Jimmy telling him, ''I *cannot endure* living with anybody--sharing the same bathroom, getting tooth brushes mixed up ... I can't stand it, and never could, and was a fool to think I could,'' a quote from Spalding. The affair was over, although slightly cushioned by the news that Duncan's last exhibition had brought in £1,600, a princely sum. Duncan was gaining in renown, which brought him new boys to fill the place Jimmy had vacated. He returned to London where he received the news of Lytton Strachey's death from stomach cancer at age 52, the end of a man exceptional in all meanings of the word. Virginia Woolf wrote that she, Vanessa and Duncan "sobbed together". This was followed by the death of Roger Fry, in his sixties, from a heart attack, another terrible blow to those who knew him well, and the *thousands* who had been faithful to and enthralled by his lectures. He too had been a wonderfully inspirational light.

Lytton by Grant and Lytton by Vanessa Bell.

All of the Bloomsbury Set distanced themselves from Keynes after his marriage, even though his ballerina wife went on to become a theatrical actress, her accent heavily Russian but her presence and talent real. They both settled into plain middle age, and Keynes neither looked nor behaved as in the past, his influence on the world stage having severely altered him. Nonetheless eternally generous to Duncan, he bestowed a yearly annuity on him in 1937, Duncan now entering his fifties.

Duncan visited Gerald Brenan in Spain, the lover of John Hope-Johnstone, the boy with whom he set out to see china on foot and turned back after 1,560 miles, mentioned in the first chapter. He was now married to an American and had two adopted children. The reader may remember that he finished his life, at age 93, in a cottage next to Hope-Johnstone's. Gerald invited him to some corridas, subject of delight for Duncan and the source of colorful paintings. Duncan and Vanessa returned to Rome where they learned that Julian had been offered a post as professor of English at the University of Wuhan in China, wasting no time in making the Dean's wife his mistress, the news of which he wrote to his mother who answered that she was always thrilled to hear about his undertakings. Civil war broke out in Spain and Julian decided to take part, promising his mother he would not engage in the actual fighting, and so it was as an ambulance driver that he died from flying bomb shrapnel. The pain of losing a child is of course the worst known to the world, and no one who had known Julian would ever overcome his loss. Vanessa filled her time by arranging a compilation of Julian's poems, essays and letters, edited by his brother Quentin, to which David Garnett added a memoir, David who had given Julian work as a book reviewer when David was literary editor of the *New Statesman*.

Julian by Duncan and Julian's photo.

Shortly afterwards Stephen Tomlin, Tommy, died at age 35, he who had been the love-interest of both Davidson brothers, who had made a sculpture of Duncan's head and had married Lytton Strachey's niece, dead of a combination of depression and alcoholism.

David Garnett visited Duncan and Vanessa to help them get through their rough patch, which led to a growing attachment to their daughter Angelica, whom Vanessa had told, following Julian's death, that she was Duncan's daughter. Then Duncan saw her leaving David's room and asked him what the hell was going on. David chose to explain himself to Vanessa: ''My love for Angelica is made up of every sort of love; it is mixed up with my love of you and Duncan and the past; but it is extremely strong and sincere, and I think unselfish,'' certainly the truth. David was still married, but his wife's breast cancer, not helped by her knowledge of what was taking place between David and Angelica, led to her death and Duncan's freedom [harsh but the truth]. Arriving home Vanessa learned that David had taken Angelica to the hospital. Surmising the reason, she demanded to know if her daughter was pregnant. David assured her that he had taken her to see a doctor only because she had a slight fever, but the animosity from both parents was so clear that David left Charleston.

In 1940 Duncan was 55 and he and Vanessa provided a welcoming home at Charleston for their children and visitors, despite war food restrictions. They were truly a couple, down to choosing, together, which seeds to plant for flowers and the vegetables that would supplement their menus. Time passed in painting, in reading, is gossip about the neighbors, in debates and political discussion, and it was certain that Duncan, increasingly bored, was increasingly ready for adventure in the form of a young lover. Quentin dropped by when he could, as did Clive Bell and David, making plans with Angelica for where they would eventually settle down. Patrick Nelson, a Jamaican, posed for Duncan in scenes Duncan loved to draw, back-stage depictions of what Duncan liked best.

Hercules and Diomedes.

Duncan and other artists represented Britain in the Venice Biennale of 1940, a huge honor and a return to a city Duncan knew well and greatly loved. Jimmy Seean showed up, and we can only hope that he and Duncan found some quality time together, though doubtful, as Venice was a center of *young* love, something Seean was game to exploit with a boy or girl his age or less. Back in London the blitzkrieg was underway, and one of Duncan's aunts was killed. David remained mostly in the capital due to Duncan's increasing hostility, Duncan who referred to him as ''that snake in the grass'', extremely sad as David Garnett had truly been the love of Duncan's life up until then. Still, the imagery of what David had experienced with him sexually, the mental imagining of what he was doing with Angelica and perhaps what David had done with Julian, were intolerable. Yet marriage became more likely as it would perhaps defuse Duncan and Vanessa's hostility, David felt, and would be proof of Angelica's love for him.

Instead of ending Part II in the Greek way, with pictures of Duncan at age 16, I have another idea of how to venerate youth, and love, no matter how crude, by presenting other works by Duncan Grant.

The veritable life and times of Duncan Grant.

PART III

It was now 1946 and Duncan was about to embark on the last leg of his life, that which he shared with Paul Roche and about which I've already written, especially in the first chapter, but as in the life of David Garnett, I didn't tell all.

They met while crossing Piccadilly, and Duncan, certainly because of his age and loss of beauty, waited for Paul to utter the first words, which he did. But among the many things I haven't revealed is the fact that Piccadilly was the center, then as today, of male prostitution, something known to all homosexuals and certainly to Duncan (4). In his mind, if Paul spoke to him it would be to earn money, something Duncan was used to after years of paying hustlers to pose nude for his paintings, and the intimacy that would intervene during the sessions.

Three drawings of Paul by Duncan.

Paul was dressed in one of those sailor suits he loved so dearly, a disguise like the ubiquitous cowboy-dressed rent-boys one finds at Times Square. The reader may remember that Paul was then a Catholic priest, a detail in itself startling when one takes into account Paul's promiscuity, his appearance in his cute uniform, his supposedly exclusive heterosexuality, and his impending sex with 61-year-old Duncan.

Paul Roche in his favorite uniform.

Paul had been born in India and educated in the classics at Ushaw College, Durham, followed by Ealing Priory day school near Hanwell, St Edmund's College and lastly the English College in Rome. He immediately posed nude for Duncan, and claimed that Duncan kissed each piece of clothing as he took it off, and each piece as he put it back on, which makes me think of an interview with Christopher Isherwood in which he was asked why he liked boys, "Because they're romantic" (9). Duncan wrote his novella *Patroclus and Narcissus* [which took place in Paris, Patroclus and Narcissus French lads], in which Duncan was Patroclus, whose ambition was to educate and bring order to the life of Narcissus, a boy who was thoroughly immoral. Whereas Montherlant, Gide and Jouhandeau (1) suffered from their disobedience of Catholic religious dogma, Paul reconciled church and sex. He was open about what he wanted and got from Duncan: "My need for sex was insatiable. He could suck or jerk me off and save me the shear tedium of girl hunting; though the girl hunting resumed the moment he left for Charleston. There was never any lovemaking in the ordinary sense between Duncan and me. And as for buggery--which is what he wanted--it was out of the question." This was the center of Paul's narcissism. Paul would allow his body to be worshipped, and in that he found perfection in Duncan, whose own beauty was increasingly less attractive, the hell we must all endure if we choose to go on living, which made Duncan appreciate Paul all the more.

Paul by Duncan.

Paul moved in with Duncan in London, and when Vanessa visited them she invited Paul--like the good sport she was--to Charleston. He, on the other hand, treated her like the grandmother she could conceivably have been, given the difference between her age and Paul's. So Charleston was out of the question, a huge weight on Duncan who wanted the boy near him at all times. [Another version suggests that Paul stayed away so as not to offend Vanessa with his and Duncan's lovemaking under her roof.]

Duncan traveled with Paul throughout Italy, and amusingly Paul, whose need for girls was obsessive and his good looks assured him a plentiful supply, wrote in Greek in his journal about the intimate details of his conquests, not knowing that Duncan had had enough Greek in school to be able to decipher the passages. Duncan was amazed by the frequency of his trysts, but was especially infuriated by Paul's absences, as he had been in Italy with Jimmy Sheean's--the absence of one's belovèd often *the* major cause of one's suffering in a love affair. Duncan tried to drown his impatience in whisky, but luckily Paul would normally be back for bed at night, and young and virile enough to share his seed with Duncan, between his lips or fingers. Despite Paul's sexual needs for women, boys nonetheless also played a part, as one boy Paul met at a swimming pool and made love to on his and Duncan's bed.

Paul had heard a great deal about Stephen Spender and asked Duncan to introduce him. Spender immediately fell for Paul, repeatedly telling him he was beautiful, "so beautiful!" [It's amazing how easily some boys will give themselves for a complement or two. In Rome Gore Vidal would stop his Jaguar convertible in the midst of a group of youths and while they admired it he would choose the best looking and say to him, "You're the most beautiful boy I've ever seen," and see what went down from there (9).] Stephen visited Duncan's studio and was surprised by the huge mirror opposite the bed, and the carnal voyeurism it implied.

In 1952 Quentin married, and his son, born in 1953, was named Julian. Paul was in baby-making mode too, getting two of his girls pregnant in the space of a few months. His son Tobit was born to a physicist, his daughter Pandora to an American that Paul decided to marry. Paul left Duncan in Regent Street where he took a bus that would take him to the quay and ship sailing to the States, wearing a Savile Row suit Duncan had offered him. Duncan was in huge distress, but it would not last long as there were still plenty of years left in the 32 he was destined to share with Paul Roche.

Roy Harrod came out with Maynard Keynes's biography in 1951, casting a major spotlight on the Bloomsbury Set, one of the most astounding brotherhoods of human beings Britain would know, Keynes the cornerstone, followed in renown by Duncan Grant whose paintings today sell for around £200,000 [$266,000]. Books, those written by Virginia Woolf, Strachey, and others, did not increase in value [except for rare editions], and a number of writers who won the Noble Prize for Literature are not even published today, or hardly so, Roger Martin du Gard, André Gide and François Mauriac, among the French, are examples of hugely popular writers back then, now largely neglected (1). In the time of Duncan Grant one could subsist on the publication of poetry, and some writers were even raised to the level of gods, like Byron, and the Isherwoods and Audens on the planet dined with the wealthy who begged for their presence, men whose literary accomplishments were such that they were accompanied by the trophies that made them the envy of the rarified world in which they gravitated: the exquisite boys they bedded. Today these same men are known for their diaries and journals, and even the fame brought to Christopher Isherwood by his novel *Cabaret* [*Goodbye to Berlin*] was in reality due to another, a genius named Bob Fosse. And woe to the student obliged to wade through *Moby Dick*, that found its public thanks to the real-life sinking of the whale boat *Essex* in 1820 [Melville's book published in 1851]. *Luck* ... often the essential ingredient of success.

The witch-hunt against homosexuals again raised its filthy head, which made Duncan wonder, with the publication of the books that pointed to his male-male relationships, if he were going to be arrested. There were the Montagu scandals at the time, which followed the Oscar Wilde disaster, all explained in my book *Christ Had His John, I Have My George, The History of British Homosexuality.*

Other biographies soon appeared and Duncan's homosexuality increasingly exposed to all. Even David Garnett published the first tomb of his memoirs, *The Golden Echo,* in 1953, the second volume, the *Flowers of the Forest,* soon to follow. News came from Paul Roche that he now had a second son, Martin, and, far more important for Duncan, assurances from Roche that he loved him. Paul began doing translations of the Greek classics, which won him success and renown. David Garnett visited Paul in America where he was teaching English at Smith College, and thanks to Paul's beauty and charm immediately fell in love with him. There was certainly no question of David's bedding the boy, as basically heterosexual Paul would have kept him at arm's length [even if boys often give in through pity, which costs them little more than a bit of semen, supplemented by the accompanying pleasure].

Vanessa had had a solo exhibition of her paintings at the Adams Gallery in 1956 and another was planned for 1961. She was choosing the pictures she was thinking of exposing when she came down with a cold that developed into bronchitis. Worried about her, Duncan and Quentin spent the afternoon in conversation, the door to Vanessa's bedroom open. At 6:00 p.m. forty years of companionship came to an end when she ceased breathing.

Paul Roche reclining

Paul Roche had received a $4,000 grant to continue his translations, and the moment he heard of Vanessa's death he wrote to Duncan that he would immediately come to London, aware that he was the only person in the world capable of lightening his burden, which was the case as Duncan was overjoyed to receive him. Vanessa's exhibition went on as scheduled and several paintings were sold.

Duncan was supposedly not sleeping with Roche out of respect for Roche's wife who came over to England with their children and stayed at Paul's father's estate. [Paul would certainly not have wanted a resumption of physical intimacy, but had Duncan requested it, Paul would probably have acquiesced out of friendship.] Duncan returned to his painting and did drawings of increasingly erotic content, showing copulation and fellatio, so many that a collection of them, *The Erotic Art of Duncan Grant*, was published in 1989, eleven years after his death. This may have given him sexual access to the boys who did the modeling for the drawings, although the majority of the drawings most certainly sprang from his memory of past experiences. Frances Partridge's son Burgo, cited in the first chapter, was on a similar wavelength with the publication of his *A History of Orgies*. Burgo married Angelica and Garnett's daughter Henrietta, seventeen, and both lived on a houseboat. As for Duncan, he continued living in Charleston, alone as Paul was in London. Vanessa's husband Clive Bell died at age 83 in 1964, the year Duncan put on an exhibition at the Wildenstein Gallery in celebration of his eightieth birthday, which brought him £5,000, nearly £100,000 today, and Vanessa's paintings steadily gained in value. His former lover the effeminate Eddy Sackville-West died in 1965 and in 1967 Angelica and David Garnett divorced.

Turnbaugh suggests that Duncan considered Paul a son and that his greatest wish was for Paul to cycle around Italy where he'd make a peasant girl pregnant and then return to London with the boy for Duncan to love and care for as his own son. As for his own liaisons, Duncan continued on, sexually active, seeking young men to pose for him, most of whom could have been his grandchildren. He was kindly and paternal, he had a sense of fun, he made them feel entirely unique and, of course, he took care of their needs, dining them and seeing they were not bereft of funds. He knew the proper way to worship a boy, and some may well have been deserving of it and as appreciative as Paul Roche had been. The ''models'' occasionally stole from him, although unlike Montherlant who was blinded in one eye by a hustler (1), Duncan never experienced violence. One lad took 100 of his paintings, enough to buy a house before he was caught, and even then Duncan put Paul to work writing letters to various authorities in an attempt to free him from prison.

In 1967 the Rye Art Gallery gave an exhibition of 101 paintings and art works produced at the Omega Workshops entitled Artists of Bloomsbury, another stone in the construction of a legend, this followed by Michael Holroyd's *Lytton Strachey* in 1968 [revamped in 1994], which not only outed Strachey, Keynes and Grant as homosexuals, but gave details that, at the time, would have made a sailor blush. Duncan was immensely offended, as more and more about what went on in the privacy of Bloomsbury bedrooms was laid bare, but the scope would still not be revealed for years, and even today has only partially been so.

Boys at play.

Duncan, 86, continued to receive visitors galore at Charleston, one of whom was a young and handsome French boy, Pierre Herreweg, heterosexual and soon to marry, who posed naked two summers in a row, perhaps allowing Duncan a few liberties, which would have been generous on the boy's part and a gift from God for Duncan. Many biographers writing on the members of the Bloomsbury Set showed up asking for interviews, and Duncan was glad for the company and the help he could give them, Duncan an inexhaustible source of information. Duncan received an honorary degree from the University of Sussex in 1973, Quentin Bell having been chosen to give the address. He traveled a great deal with Paul, to France, Italy, Turkey, Scotland and Tangier, always Paul's idea to get him out and about. He painted. He read. And he continued to give exhibitions.

Paul moved to Charleville to care for him and was there when he came down with bronchial pneumonia. Roche and Duncan's love had been the closest, the deepest, the truest of friendships, and Roche closes the chapter on their lives in this way: ''I could see that he was in a very bad way, breathing heavily.... Dr Cooper said to me, 'I can't save him this time, he's too far gone, and it's much better to let him go'. So I agreed to that. Duncan lay on the bed.... I came up to him the night before he died... This is what I think I said, or the gist of it.... 'Duncan, you have nothing to worry about, whatever you have done in life that you are sorry for, God loves you, whatever you've done, He loves you. You don't have to worry about anything. You're in His hands, and so you can sleep peacefully and everything is ok.... Don't think that God is angry with anything.... He's not, He loves you.' Duncan was incapable of speaking ... so I quietly left the room.... When I came back in the morning ... I realised Duncan was dead. That was an enormous shock to me.... I went to Firle to be at the funeral, but I suddenly found that I couldn't stand, every time I stood up I simply collapsed onto the floor.'' Duncan died at age 93, Paul followed in 2007 at age 91.

SOURCES

1- See my book *French Homosexuality*.
2- See my book *Boarding School Homosexuality*.
3- See my book *TROY*.
4- See my book *Christ Had His John, I Have My George, The History of British Homosexuality*.
5- See my book *Greek Homosexuality*.
6- See my book *SPARTA*.
7- See my book *Roman Homosexuality*.
8- See my book *John [Jack] Nickolson*.
9- See my book *American Homosexual Giants*.
10- See my book *German Homosexuality*.
11- See my book *The Belle Epoque*.
12- See my book *Alcibiades*.
13- See my autobiography, *Michael Hone, His World, His Loves*.

Aldrich and Wotherspoon, *Who's Who in Gay and Lesbian History*, 2001.
Andress, David, *The Terror*, 2005.
Baker Simon, *Ancient Rome*, 2006.
Barber, Richard, *The Devil's Crown--Henry II and Sons*, 1978.
Barber, Stanley, *Alexandros*, 2010.
Barré, Jean-Luc, *François Mauriac, Biographie intime*, 2009.
Bawlf, Samuel, *The Secret Voyage of Sir Francis Drake*, 2003.
Beachy, Robert, *Gay Berlin*, 2014. Marvelous.
Bicheno, Hugh, *Vendetta*, 2007.
Bierman, John, *Dark Safari, Henry Morton Stanley*, 1990.
Blanchard, Jean-Vincent, *Éminence, Cardinal Richelieu*.
Bret, Davis, *Trailblazers*, 2009.
Burg, B.R., *Gay Warriors*, 2002.
Bury and Meiggs, *A History of Greece*, 1975.
Calimach, Andrew, *Lover's Legends*, 2002.
Caro, Robert, *The Years of Lyndon Johnson*, Vol. 4, 2012.
Carter, William, *Proust in Love*, 2006.
Cartledge, Paul, *Alexander the Great*, 2004.
Cartledge, Paul, *Sparta and Lakonia*, 1979.
Cartledge, Paul, *The Spartans*, 2002.
Cate, Curtis, *Friedrich Nietzsche*, 2003.

Cawthorne, Nigel, *Sex Lives of the Popes*, 1996
Cellini, Benvenuto, *The Autobiography of Benvenuto Cellini*.
Ceram, C.W., *Gods, Graves and Scholars*, 1951.
Chamberlin, E.R. *The Fall of the House of Borgia*, 1974.
Clark, Christopher, *Iron Kingdom*, 2006.
Clerc, Thomas, *Maurice Sachs, Le Désoeuvré*, 2005.
Cloulas, Ivan, *The Borgia*, 1989
Cocteau, Jean, *Le Livre Blanc*, Livre de Poche 1999.
Cooper, John, *The Queen's Agent*, 2011.
Crompton, Louis, *Byron and Greek Love*, 1985.
Crompton, Louis, *Homosexuality and Civilization*, 2003.
Crouch, David, *William Marshal*, 1990.
Crowley, Roger, *Empires of the Sea*, 2008. Marvelous.
Cruickshank, John, *Montherland*, 1964.
Curtis Cate, *Friedrich Nietzsche*, 2002.
Davenport-Hines, Richard, *The Seven Lives of Maynard Keynes*, 2015.
Davidson, James, *Courtesans and Fishcakes*, 1998.
Davidson, James, *The Greeks and Greek Love*, 2007.
Dover K.J. *Greek Homosexuality*, 1978.
Duby, George, *William Marshal*, 1985.
Eisler, Benita, *BYRON Child of Passion, Fool of Fame*, 2000. Wonderful.
Erlanger, Philippe, *Buckingham*, 1951.
Erlanger, Philippe, *The King's Minion*, 1901.
Everitt Anthony, *Augustus*, 2006
Everitt Anthony, *Cicero*, 2001.
Everitt Anthony, *Hadrian*, 2009
Fagles, Robert, *The Iliad*, 1990.
Gidel, Henry, *Cocteau*, 2009.
Gillman, Peter and Leni, *The Wildest Dream*, 2000.
Gilmore, John, *Laid Bare*, 1997.
Gilmore, John, *Live Fast—Die Young*, 1997.
Goldsworthy Adrian, *Caesar*, 2006
Goodwin, Robert, *SPAIN*, 2015.
Gore-Browne, Robert, *Lord Bothwell*, 1937
Graham-Dixon, Andrew, *Caravaggio* 2010. Fabulous.
Graham, Robb, *Strangers*, 2003.
Grant Michael, *History of Rome*, 1978
Graves, Robert, *Greek Myths*, 1955.
Grazia, Sebastian de, *Machiavelli in Hell*, 1989.
Grèce, Michel de, *Le Vol du Régent*, 2008.
Halperin David M. *One Hundred Years of Homosexuality*, 1990
Harris Robert, *Imperium*, 2006
Herodotus, *The Histories*, Penguin Classics.

Hesiod and Theognis, Penguin Classics, 1973.

Hibbert, Christopher, *Florence, the Biography of a City,* 1993.

Hibbert, Christopher, *The Borgias and Their Enemies,* 2009.

Hibbert, Christopher, *The Days of the French Revolution,* 1981.

Hibbert, Christopher, *The Great Mutiny India 1857,* 1978. Fabulous.

Hibbert, Christopher, *The Rise and Fall of the House of Medici,* 1974.

Hicks, Michael, *Richard III,* 2000.

Hine, Daryl, *Puerilities,* 2001.

Hirst, Michael, *The Tudors,* 2007.

Hochschild, Adam, *King Leopold's Ghost,* 1999.

Hofler, Robert, *Party Animals,* 2010.

Holland Tom, *Rubicon,* 2003

Holland, Tom, *Persian Fire,* 2005.

Holroyd, Michael, *Lytton Strachey,* 1994.

Hughes, Robert, *Rome,* 2011.

Hughes, Robert, *The Fatal Shore,* 1987.

Hutchinson, Robert, *House of Treason,* 2009.

Hutchinson, Robert, *Thomas Cromwell,* 2007.

Jack Belinda, *Beatrice's Spell,* 2004.

James, Callum, *My Dear KJ...* edited by James, 2015.

Jeal, Tim, *STANLEY,* 2007. All of Jeal's books are must-reads.

Johnson, Marion, *The Borgias,* 1981.

Jouhandeau, Marcel, *Ecrits secrets,* 1988.

Knights, Sarah, *Bloomsbury's Outside, A Life of David Garnett,* 2015.

Lacey, Robert, *Henry VIII,* 1972.

Lacy, Robert, *Sir Walter Ralegh,* 1973.

Leeming, David, *Stephen Spender,* 1999.

Lubkin, Gregory, *A Renaissance Court,* 1994.

Lyons, Mathew, *The Favourite,* 2011.

Malye, Jean, *La Véritable Histore d'Alcibiade,* 2009.

Manchester, William, *A World Lit Only By Fire,* 1993.

Marchand, Leslie, *Byron,* 1971.

Martin,Brian Joseph, *Napoleonic Friendship,* 2011.

Martines, Lauro, *April Blood-Florence and the Plot against the Medici,* 2003.

McCann, Graham, *Rebel Males,* 1991.

McLynn, Frank, *Richard and John, Kings of War,* 2007. Fabulous.

McLynn, *Marcus Aurelius,* 2009

McLynn, *STANLEY, The making of an African explorer,* 1989.

Meier, Christian, *Caesar,* 1996.

Merrick/Sibalis, *Homosexuality in French History and Culture,* 2012.

Meyer, G.J. *The Borgias, The Hidden History,* 2013.

Meyer, G.J. *The Tudors,* 2010.

Meyer, Jack, *Alcibiades,* 2009.

Miles Richard, *Ancient Worlds*, 2010.

Miles Richard, *Carthage Must be Destroyed*, 2010

Miller, David, *Richard the Lionheart*, 2003.

Minichiello, Victor and John Scott, *Male Sex Work and Society*, 2014.

Mitford, Nancy, *Frederick the Great*, 1970.

Moore Lucy, *Amphibious Thing*, 2000.

Nicholl, Charles, *The Reckoning*, 2002.

Noel, Gerard, *The Renaissance Popes*, 2006.

Norton, Rictor, *My Dear Boy*, Love Letters edited by Norton, 1998.

Oosterhuis and Kennedy, *Homosexuality and Male Bonding*, 1991.

Opper, Thorsten, *Hadrian, Empire and Conflict*, 2008.

Pearce, Joseph, *The Unmasking of Oscar Wilde*, 2000.

Pernot, Michel, *Henri III, Le Roi Décrié*, 2013, Excellent book.

Pernot, Michel, *Henri III, Le Roi Décrié*, 2013, Excellent book.

Peyrefitte, Roger, *Alexandre*, 1979.

Peyrefitte, Roger, *Propos secrets,* Volumes 1 and 2, 1977, 1980.

Plutarch's Lives, Modern Library.

Pollard, J., *Warwick the Kingmaker*, 2007.

Polybius, *The Histories*

Reed, Jeremy, *The Dilly*, 2014.

Reid, B.L., *The Lives of Roger Casement*, 1976.

Reston, James, *Warriors of God, Richard and the Crusades*, 2001.

Revenin, Régis, *Homosexualité et Prostitution Maculines à Paris*, 2005.

Rice, Edward, *Captain Sir Richard Francis Burton*, 1990.

Ridley, Jasper, *The Tudor Age*, 1998.

Robb, Graham, *Rimbaud*, 2000. Superb.

Rocco, Antonio, *Alcibiade Enfant à l'Ecole*, 1630.

Rocke, Michael, *Forbidden Friendships*, 1996. Fabulous/indispensible.

Romans Grecs et Latin, Gallimard, 1958.

Ross, Charles, *Richard III,* 1981.

Rouse, W.H.D., Homer's *The Iliad*, 1938.

Ruggiero, Guido, *The Boundaries of Eros*, 1985.

Sabatini, Rafael, *The Life of Cesare Borgia*, 1920.

Saint Bris, Gonzague, *Henri IV,* 2009.

Saslow, James, *Ganymede in the Renaissance*, 1986.

Schama, Simon, *Citizens* 1989.

Scurr, Ruth, *Fatal Purity*, 2007.

Setz, Wolfram, *The Sins of the Cities of the Plain*, 1881.

Shapiro, James, *1599*, 2005.

Sharaf, Myron, *Fury on Earth: A Biography of Wilhelm Reich*, 1983.

Sheridan, Alan, *André Gide*, 1999.

Simonetta, Marcello, *The Montefeltro Conspiracy*, 2008. Wonderful.

Sipriot, Pierre, *Montherlant sans masque*, 1982.

Skidelsky, Robert, *The Essential Keynes*, 2016.
Skidmore, Chris, *Bosworth*, 1988.
Skidmore, Chris, *Death and the Virgin*, 2010.
Solnon, Jean-Fançois, *Henry III*, 1996.
Spalding, Frances, *Duncan Grant*, 1997.
Stewart, Alan, *The Cradle King, A Life of James VI & I*, 2003.
Strathern, Paul, *The Medici, Godfathers of the Renaissance*, 2003. Superb.
Summers, Julia, *Fearless on Everest*, 2009.
Tamagne, Florence, *A History of Homosexuality in Europe*, 2004.
Tuchman, Barbara, *A Distant Mirror*, 1978.
Turnbaugh, Douglas Blair, *Duncan Grant*, 1987.
Unger Miles, *Magnifico, The Brilliant Life and Violent Time.s*
Unger, Miles, *Machiavelli*, 2008.
Vaughan, Richard, *John the Fearless*, 1973.
Vernant, Jean-Pierre, *Mortals and Immortals*, 1991.
Violet, Bernard, *Les Mystères Delon*, 2000.
Warren, W.L., *Henry II*, 1973.
Weir, Alison, *Eleanor of Aquitaine*, 1999. Weir is a fabulous writer.
Whyte, Kenneth, *The Uncrowned King*, 2008.
Wikipedia: Research today is impossible without the aid of this monument.
Williams Craig A. *Roman Homosexuality*, 2010.
Williams John, *Augustus*, 1972
Wilson, Derek, *The Uncrowned Kings of England*, 2005.
Worthington, Ian, *Philip II of Macedonia*, 2008.
Wright, Ed, *History's Greatest Scandals*, 2006.
Wroe, Ann, *Perkin, A Story of Deception*, 2003. Fabulous
Xenophon, *A History of My Time*s, Penguin Classics.
Xenophon, *The Persian Expedition*, 1949.
Zachks, Richard, *History Laid Bare*, 1994.

INDEX

Many of the people in this book are listed as *passim* because they are present from beginning to end. Others, for example Frances Partridge, are designated in this fashion, Frances Partridge 124-129, meaning that the person appears between these pages, but *not* necessarily on *every* page.

Made in United States
North Haven, CT
13 September 2023

41519104R00085